RENEWING OUR DAYS

To the memory of Avriel Butovsky ז"ל

1959-1993

RENEWING OUR DAYS

Montreal Jews in the Twentieth Century

EDITED BY

Ira Robinson and Mervin Butovsky

Véhicule Press

MONTRÉAL

A DOSSIER QUÉBEC BOOK

Published with the assistance of The Canada Council

The quotation on page 119 by Judith Davis appeared in *Essays in the Social Scientific Study of Judaism and Jewish Society* (Concordia University), and is reprinted with permission of Concordia University.

Cover photograph by R.E. Fleischman, courtesy of the Canadian Jewish Congress National Archives. Beginning of the construction/conversion of a building for the Jewish Peretz School, 120 Duluth St., 1942. The banner reads: "Congratulations! Honour to the builders! In our youth is our hope!

Interior design and imaging: Simon Garamond
Printing: Imprimerie d'Édition Marquis Ltée

Dépôt légal, Bibliothèque nationale du Québec and the
National Library of Canada, fourth quarter 1995.

CANADIAN CATALOGUING IN PUBLICATION DATA

Main entry under title:
Renewing our days : Montreal Jews in the twentieth century

(Dossier Québc series)
ISBN 1-55065-062-9

1. Jews–Quebec (Province)–Montréal–History–20th century. 2. Jews–Quebec (Province)–Montréal–Social conditions. 3. Canadian literature–Quebec (Province)–Montréal–Jewish authors–History and criticism. I. Robinson, Ira, 1951- II. Butovksy, Mervin III. Series.

FC2947.9.J4R45 1995 971.4'28004924 C95-900279-0
F1054.5.M89J4 1995

Published by Véhicule Press, P.O.B. 125, Place du Parc Station,
Montreal, Quebec H2W 2M9.
Distributed by GDS, 30 Lesmill Rd., Don Mills, Ontario M3B 2T6

Printed in Canada on acid-free paper.

CONTENTS

Preface

This volume, like our previous collaboration, *An Everyday Miracle: Yiddish Culture in Montreal* (1990), grew out of an academic conference held at Montreal's Jewish Public Library entitled "Tur Malka: the Jewish Experience in Montreal," and it took place in May, 1992.

The editors hope that *Renewing Our Days*, like *An Everyday Miracle*, will help stimulate interest in the study of Quebec and Canadian Jewry. In so doing we will also be furthering the purposes of Concordia University's Chair in Quebec and Canadian Jewish Studies, with which we are both affiliated as research associates.

We are pleased to to acknowledge the financial support this conference received from Concordia University, the Jewish Public Library and the Social Sciences and Humanities Research Council of Canada.

Introduction

MONTREAL JEWRY in the twentieth century has yet to find its definitive historian. At least in part this is because scholars who have examined the Jews of Montreal have been understandably influenced by the fact that, for most of the history of the Jews in Canada, Montreal has constituted *the* place where Canadian Jews have enjoyed their greatest numerical concentration as well as cultural creativity. There was, therefore, a tendency to write general histories of Canadian Jewry incorporating much Montreal material. Montreal as a separate community was thus somewhat neglected. Studies of Jews in Canada, as well as more specific contributions to the study of Montreal Jewry, such as those of David Rome in the successive volumes of *Canadian Jewish Archives*, have been of tremendous use to scholars attempting to understand the Montreal Jewish experience. However, for the most part, these studies tend to illuminate their specific subjects and leave aside the examination of the broader picture of the Montreal Jewish experience. This introduction cannot pretend to fill this gap in any meaningful way. Nonetheless, in order to be able to intelligently approach the specificities of the articles contained in the present volume concerning aspects of the twentieth century experience of Jews in Montreal, it is necessary that at least a brief sketch of the social, religious and literary history of the Jews of Montreal be attempted.

Context

Montreal Jews need to be understood in the context of the vagaries of Jewish life in the nineteenth and twentieth centuries. Previously, Jews had constituted a group by and large relegated by both law and custom to the margins of the societies in which they lived. However modernity saw the Jews presented with the prospect of equal civil and even political rights in the countries they called home. These rights, however, came at the explicit price of the abandonment of the Jews' status as a distinct group governed by its own laws and customs. Modernity was thus both a promise and a threat for the Jews. For one thing, it meant that Jews were, at least in theory, no longer going to be coerced into being Jewish. Starting in the late eighteenth century, adherence to Judaism would become an essentially voluntary act and Jews were free to experiment with different ways of being Jewish. On the other hand, this freedom would come at the price of the coherence of Jews and Judaism. It is at this point that the question of "Who is a Jew?" as well as the modern "Jewish problem" came into prominence as never before.

This new freedom as well as its attendant problems was in evidence first of all in Western European Jewish communities, particularly in Germany. However it was in North America, especially the United States, which did not possess the same established communal institutions to serve as a brake upon experimentation that Europe possessed, and where the presence of overt anti-Semitism was somewhat less obtrusive, that this freedom was often carried to its utmost limits. Canada's experience, in this instance as in others, was at one and the same time "American" and "European." On the one hand, Canadian Jews were free to experiment with new ways of doing things. However this experimentation was always limited by British as well as French Canadian traditions of respect for ancient and venerable institutions.

Jews were of historic importance for the development of the Canadian polity in that they constituted the first group of non-Christian European settlers to establish itself in Canada. Jews thus constituted the opening wedge for the still ongoing debate on whether Canadian society was meant to be based on a multicultural pluralism as opposed to the "two founding peoples" model. In Canadian society, and particularly in Quebec, Jews were especially important as testers of the limits of societal acceptance of "others" in a climate of opinion which tended to take the nexus between Christianity and civilization for granted.

The Development of a Community

Founded in the seventeenth century, Montreal was an outpost of a French regime which had set Catholic religious purity as its goal and did not wish to have alternative religious expressions—whether Protestant or Jewish—present in its colonies. Though there were Jews involved in the French colonial trade, and though individual Jews are said to have visited New France, they were not allowed to live an openly Jewish lifestyle and most certainly Jewish communal life would not have been allowed to develop.

It was the British conquest of Quebec in 1759 which brought about the beginnings of Jewish life in Quebec. Jews who arrived shortly thereafter formed the first Jewish community in Montreal and founded Congregation Shearith Israel in 1768.

Even though they were relatively few in numbers, the Jews of Quebec, like Jews elsewhere in the British empire, possessed greater civil and economic rights than Jews enjoyed in most other European lands. So much so that there were some among them who, by the beginning of the nineteenth century, aspired to political rights as well. These rights, however, were to be contested by those who felt that the right to vote and to be elected to a legislature or appointed to a magistracy should be restricted to those who professed Christianity. These opponents of Jewish political rights took seriously the traditional notion that Jews constituted a separate nation and could not possibly be counted as an integral part of any polity but their own. It was the nascent Jewish presence in the political life of North America which raised the question, not completely answered to this day, whether the countries of North America were in fact "Christian" or not.

Thus when, in 1807, Ezekiel Hart was elected to the Legislative Assembly of Lower Canada from Trois-Rivières, he was denied the right to take his seat on the grounds of his Jewishness. Not until 1832 would Jews in British North America, well in advance of Jews in the Mother Country, be granted this right.

Although a number of individuals and families from among these earliest settlers did achieve positions of financial and political prominence and most identified themselves as Jews, they were too few in number to establish the sort of cohesive communal institutions that could act as a brake against cultural assimilation, intermarriage, and eventual disappearance as Jews.

In the nineteenth century, Jewish immigration to British North America did not cease, but it certainly did not increase with the vigor that it did in the United States. Thus at the time of Confederation, there were barely a thousand Jews in the Canadian population while the Jewish population of the United States numbered in the hundreds of thousands. The main source of Jewish immigration to North America until the latter part of the nineteenth century came from the German lands, and there was relatively little German-Jewish immigration to Canada. Since German Jews were behind the rise to prominence of Reform Judaism in the United States, this was one reason why Reform Judaism did not develop in Canada the way it had south of the border. Another reason was the English influence, previously mentioned. Because of this, Canadian Jews tended to be more traditional in their religious practices than their American cousins. Furthermore, in Montreal the predominant Christian denomination was Roman Catholic. There was much less impetus to change the language and mode of Jewish prayer when the Catholics maintained their ancient rituals and liturgical language. Reform, when it did appear in Montreal, as elsewhere in Canada, was largely an American import.

Prior to the major emigration of Jews from Eastern Europe, which started in earnest in the 1880s, the Jews of Montreal numbered in the hundreds. In the 1871 census, the first after Confederation, there were 409 Jews in Montreal, organized in two synagogues. Shearith Israel, the Spanish and Portuguese Synagogue, originally founded in the eighteenth century, had consolidated its position as the major congregation of the city. It retained the Sephardic rituals though its community at the time had relatively few ethnic Sephardic Jews. It prospered under the able spiritual leadership of Abraham de Sola. A second congregation had been founded in 1846 for those who wished to pray according to the religious customs of the Ashkenazim. It was called the Synagogue of English, German and Polish Jews, later to be named Shaar Hashomayim. A Young Men's Hebrew Benevolent Society, founded in 1863 (to be renamed the Baron de Hirsch Institute in 1900) and a Ladies Hebrew Benevolent Society, founded in 1877, rounded out the communal activities of Montreal Jews in providing succor for indigent Jews, who were often encouraged to settle elsewhere than in Montreal.

The Great Eastern European Emigration

In the late nineteenth and early twentieth centuries, poverty and persecution in Eastern Europe accompanied by liberal conditions and economic opportunity in the New World caused a massive emigration of Jews to North America. Most of these Jews came to the United States, but enough came to Canada to mark a turning point in Canadian Jewish history. Those who wound up in the Dominion of Canada were not always at first cognizant of the fact that the part of "Amerike" in which they were living was in fact a different country from the United States. In Montreal they succeeded in transforming a relatively small, largely acculturated community into one of the most prominent Jewish communities in the North American diaspora.

Eastern European Jews coming to Montreal managed to effect a demographic revolution. There were 6975 Jews in Montreal in 1901 compared to 409 thirty years previously. By the time the mass Eastern European emigration to Canada had been halted, in 1931, Montreal's Jewish population had increased to 58,032. Jews at that time made up the third largest ethnic/national group in the city after the English and the French. The majority of these immigrants derived from the Pale of Settlement—an area that includes parts of present-day Russia, Poland, the Ukraine and Lithuania—as well as the Austro-Hungarian Empire and Romania, where Jews had resided for over a thousand years and had fashioned a coherent religious civilization. By the mid-nineteenth century however, this autonomous Jewish society was rent by external oppression and severe internal social and religious conflicts. Contending religious, social, and political ideologies, a consequence of the Jewish confrontation with the modern world, opened fissures within the once unified belief system, causing profound disruptions within the traditional societies. At about the same time, violent anti-Jewish outbreaks in Russia and Romania —to which the government often seemed to acquiesce—as well as a stagnant economy throughout Eastern Europe raised alarm in the community about its own survival. These circumstances—the internal disarray and the external persecution—set off a vast migration of Jews seeking a better future for themselves and their children. The turbulence of this disruption brought millions of Jews, as part of one of the greatest demographic movements in history, to North America and resulted in a large increase in the number of Jews in Canada and, in particular, in the burgeoning metropolis of Montreal.

This enormous influx of Jewish immigrants in a relatively brief period changed the complexion of the Montreal Jewish experience decisively. It meant, first of all, that the older, relatively more acculturated Jewish community was simply overwhelmed demographically and culturally by the new immigrants. Members of the more established community indeed attempted and in some respects succeeded in asserting their communal leadership, particularly with respect to relations with the government and the larger Canadian society, by utilizing their economic clout and selectively coopting some of the leaders of the Eastern European community. However their lesser numbers made them relatively less successful in these efforts than was the case in the United States, where the German Jews had established a sufficient demographic and institutional basis to withstand the challenges of the Eastern European immigration to a greater extent.

What were the ways in which a tradition-bound Eastern European people met the challenge of modernity that confronted them in the new world? The challenge involved the Jews' distinctive identity and their desire to retain certain essential aspects of that identity—at the same time as they sought full participation in the social, political, and cultural life of Canadian society. Because the traditional legacy they had brought with them from their countries of origin, in which most Jews still lived a premodern Jewish lifestyle, was often incompatible with the cultural norms that prevailed in North America, the process of cultural adaptation often meant a departure from past customs and their replacement with new modes of behavior and belief. Accommodation to the new conditions, even by those most resistant to the way of life offered by the new country, resulted in the attenuation and even abandonment of many former values and practices. Thus the question faced by that generation of Jewish immigrants as indeed by every community of new immigrants as they assessed their future prospects in the host culture was: How to assure the continuity of their distinctive religio-ethnic identity within the context of a society which had scant respect for or understanding of the civilization they had brought with them?

Did the Jews of Montreal create their own culture? As we will see, the answer is affirmative. Ultimately the newcomers were forced to create their own cultural space between the two founding cultures of Canada.

What made this process possible was the fact that they brought with them and sought to preserve a common language (or languages) and a sense of belonging to a distinct nation—comprising both religious and secular forms of association. As previously noted, Jews from Eastern-Europe came from many different countries and consequently employed the vernaculars of the majority cultures among whom they lived. However their sense of peoplehood, which transcended their national origins, was enhanced by the use of distinctive Jewish languages which expressed their bond of collective identity and common historical fate. Jews of Eastern-Europe, like Jews everywhere, relied on two different but interrelated linguistic practices. Hebrew, the sacred tongue, language of ancient Israel, was privileged as the medium of religious discourse, worship, and liturgy. Yiddish, the folk vernacular, functioned as the expressive colloquial speech of home, street, workplace and market. Its hybrid construction relied on the Hebrew alphabet, but incorporated Medieval German diction, grammar, and syntax, with numerous words and phrases absorbed from other European languages. When a secular bellelettristic Jewish literature emerged in the nineteenth century, writers, who were usually bilingual, relied on the popular Yiddish in order to communicate with their mass readership. Most of the East-European Jews who settled in Montreal were Yiddish-speaking and despite the diversity of national origins, their common tongue confirmed their sense of belonging to a distinct nation.

In addition to the bond of common languages which was a powerful factor in the ethnic cohesion of the Jews, other potent factors, primarily the ancient Judaic belief system, also functioned to unify the disparate sectors of the community. The Orthodox sector of the community brought to their new environment age-old patterns of belief and authority, and immediately set about transplanting their religious customs and practices to the new setting. Synagogues, schools and yeshivot, kosher butchers and bakers, and many other agencies catering to the needs of traditional Jews, soon made their appearance on Montreal streets. For the high proportion of immigrants who considered themselves to be "secular" and no longer complied with religious practices, the memory of earlier customs and childhood associations often induced a nostalgic attitude toward the faith they had abandoned—even as they sought new forms for the expression of their ancient heritage. Being "secular" in those years meant finding a replacement for what were considered to be the outmoded ways of the past, adapting new forms which were located in the arena of modern, humanistic culture, though still expressed in the Yiddish language. In politics, social organizations, art, literature, and education, they found rich and inviting fields of endeavour which held out the promise of full participation in the modern world they now inhabited.

For a number of decades following their arrival in Montreal, the ambition to recreate something of a self-sufficient Yiddish society on the shores of the St. Lawrence, seemed to some a real possibility. The great majority of the newcomers lived and worked within a well-defined area of the city. Clustered around the "Main"—St. Lawrence Boulevard—which served as a recognizable border separating the French-Catholic eastern section of the city from the English-Protestant western districts, the Jews formed a distinct enclave—a third solitude—between these major components of the city's population. Neither of the majority religio-linguistic groups was enthusiastic about the arrival of large numbers of Jewish immigrants, but the Jews massively turned to the English-speaking society for their models in the acculturation process, adopting the English language and the Protestant school system as their means of integrating into Canadian society. The Jews' association with the Anglo-Protestant enclave rather that the French-Catholic population was to have far-reaching consequences for their political future in Quebec, and a brief description of the determining factors that prompted that choice might be in order here since it will help explain why the post-Yiddish cultural activities of the Jews of Montreal were almost exclusively rendered in English, rather than the language of Quebec's majority.

The first of these factors concerned religion and the Jews' historic relationship with the Christian church—whether Orthodox or Roman Catholic. The experience of Europe caused them to be deeply suspicious and fearful of the Church, and to see its teachings as a main instigator of anti-Semitism. In Quebec, they found Catholic education mainly in the hands of the religious orders, conducted in accordance with Christian doctrine. This school system based on Catholic teachings (and taught by priests and nuns) clearly seemed to exclude the Jews. By comparison, the Protestant school system whose religiosity was relatively less obtrusive, proved more accommodating and, despite strong internal opposition and an intense debate lasting decades, the Protestant School Board eventually saw to the education of Montreal's Jewish children. In addition, Catholic clergy were prominent in the anti-immigration movements of the province. There was ample evidence that many of the clergy and Catholic lay-organizations were in the forefront of political demands for the cessation of immigration (Lionel Groulx was only the most vocal figure in this cause), and the immigrants' estrangement from the society that espoused these causes was self-protective and realistic.

Secondly, the socio-economic landscape of the immigrant neighbourhoods encouraged the Jews in their choice. Their immediate neighbours in the working-class slums and ghettos were the French Canadian poor. In many cases the French-Canadian working-class was hostile to the intrusion of "foreigners" in their districts and expressed their animosity in violent altercations—rare is the Jewish child who did not suffer a beating by local toughs. On the other hand, the English Canadians, remotely ensconced in the western parts of the city, demonstrably occupied leadership positions in the city: in trade and commerce, the professions, and public institutions. They thus appeared as models to immigrants seeking economic improvement and social advance. It must also be remembered that the earlier Jewish settlers, precursors to the later waves of migration, were mainly Jews from English-speaking countries, England or the United States. They comprised the established communal leadership in the first decades of the great immigration and their presence was an influential determinant for cultural adaptation to English.

The third factor was the contrasting conceptions of the mother-countries—England and France—in the minds of the new immigrants to Montreal. Throughout the nineteenth century Jews of Eastern-Europe regarded England as a beacon of enlightenment and political freedom. In contrast to the oppressive autocracies of their native lands, English parliamentary democracy held out the promise of equality under the law and considerable tolerance for non-Christian forms of belief. English political figures, philosophers, and writers were lauded by the Jews in the Russian Pale. France, despite its reputation as the founding nation of republicanism and individual civil rights, bore the stigma of the infamous Dreyfus case of 1894. That trial and the false charges of treason brought against the only Jewish member of the French general staff, had sent shock waves through the Jewish world and strongly influenced Jewish attitudes, including their assumptions about French-speaking Quebec.

In cultural terms, the relative linguistic and religious isolation of the Jews in Montreal ironically proved to be a positive condition in encouraging the establishment of a well-knit autonomous community life. Finding little encouragement to integrate with either of the dominant groups, the immigrants set about organizing the kind of institutions and cultural activities that would answer their needs. Drawing on the resources of their European experience, within a few short years they created a host of cultural, social, and political institutions, a veritable network that supported and sustained a vibrant community life for the next several decades. Among the most significant cultural agencies were the daily Yiddish newspaper *Keneder Odler* (The Canadian Eagle), the Jewish Public Library, elementary and high schools of various ideological persuasions which gave instruction in Yiddish and Hebrew at first supplementary to the instruction of the Protestant school system and later on including instruction in secular subjects as well along with English and French, a large number of synagogues, theatrical groups, literary societies, adult education courses, and teacher-training seminars. Social needs were met by an integrated network of health and welfare agencies that included hospitals and clinics, orphanages, homes for the aged, free loan societies, and community welfare organizations. All of these were, at least theoretically, united in the 1920s in a Jewish Community Council (*Vaad Ha-Ir*). In addition, a host of political parties and factions represented the full range of ideological positions in the community, including anarchism, socialism, communism, Zionism, trade unionism, middle-class benevolent societies, Liberal party supporters, Bundists, and many other vocal groups.

The presence of this formidable array of social, political, educational, religious, and welfare institutions gave Montreal Jewry a unique standing in North America. Beyond New York city, with its millions of Jews, Montreal was noted by many as the city with the richest quality of Jewish life on the continent. That special prominence was clearly the result of efforts of a select band of individuals who had dedicated themselves to the task of preserving *Yiddishkayt*—Yiddish culture—in the new environment of Montreal. These devoted individuals were drawn from the ranks of diverse professions and occupations: schoolteachers and educational administrators, editors and publishers, bakers and seamstresses, poets and novelists, manufacturers and businessmen, religious leaders, lawyers and insurance brokers. What they had in common was the fierce desire to conserve and reconstruct the essential elements of their remembered European lives, and to resist the siren-song of cultural assimilation in the engulfing homogeneity of North America.

In this *kulturkampf* they sought to counter the lure of assimilation with their own weapons of cultural nationalism. Primarily, Yiddish was to serve as the bulwark against the intrusion of alien creeds, and to this end their schools and library, literary periodicals and debates, outpourings of poetry and novels, were considered ammunition in the desperate resistance against the anticipated cultural loss. For a short time it seemed as though their endeavours might prove effective; the vigour of Yiddish literary creativity gave the impression of cultural vitality and futurity. In the poetry of J.I.Segal, Ida Maze, M. Shaffir, A.S. Shkolnikoff, Sholem Shtern—later to be augmented by post-World War II immigrants such as the renowned Melech Ravitch, Rachel

Korn, and Mordechai Husid—Yiddish readers were offered authentic accounts of the modern Jewish experience by powerful voices, a body of literature that conveyed something of the travail that was Jewish history in the twentieth century. The persistent theme of these poets was exile. The act of being uprooted from natal regions stimulated their imaginations and, (like the English literary modernists Yeats, Pound, and Eliot) compelled them to envisage the shattered present in terms of the memorialized past. So completely absorbing was their sense of uprootedness and dislocation, that few were ever able to deal with the reality of their Canadian lives—to depict its geography, climate, seasons—which entered their poetry only infrequently.

Among the novelists and short story writers too, their fiction mostly concentrated on the early formative stages of personal development in remembered Europe rather than depictions of the new world to which fate and history had assigned them. It was the "old country" that was constantly foregrounded—the world of recollected custom, youth, and family—an idyllic setting of a lost paradise now irrevocably destroyed. In the fiction and fictive memoirs as such writers as Yehuda Elberg, Chava Rosenfarb, and Yaacov Zipper, the tension between memory and history is graphically enacted. Only on occasion are they able to disengage themselves from the burden of the past in order to contend with the uninviting present. A similar problematic affected the work of the educators and cultural activists. Their often valiant struggle to organize and finance a school system that would offer Yiddish and Hebrew as the foundation studies of the curriculum could not withstand the pressures of acculturation. Educators like Shloime Wiseman, Yaacov Zipper, Shimshon Dunsky, and Melech Magid were tireless in their efforts to imbue their students with a sense of the cultural worth of Judaism and Jewishness. To their enormous credit, they sought to combine secular studies with respect for traditional forms, and their legacy is witnessed in the present-day vitality of the institutions they founded. Yet the utopian plans they conceived for the conservation of a Yiddish cultural world must be deemed incomplete, or even unrealizable, given the conditions they faced.

Despite the efforts of these idealistic Yiddishists, the attempt to hold back the tide of English Canadian culture proved futile. A younger generation, eager to participate in the bounty of full citizenship, found themselves adopting the new modes of thought and conduct which encouraged the spurning of the archaic ways of home and synagogue. In the simple and desirable act of attending public schools the children of immigrants acquired the linguistic capacity which both outpaced and alienated them from their parents. Encouraged by parents to further themselves through education, they ironically found in the new knowledge a secular replacement for the abandoned beliefs of home. And the resultant conflict between the generations was to become the prime source and subject of creativity when the children of the Yiddish-speaking immigrants came to set down their stories in poetry, drama, and fiction.

And, of course, the children set down their stories in English. With the acquisition of the new language the new generation was able to redefine their relationship to the past and to gain entry to the broader Canadian cultural landscape. In the very act of representing their lives as Jews in Montreal they helped expand the boundaries of the national literature so that it could begin to accommodate the new urban-ethnic dimensions of Canadian society.

Jews and Jewish Culture in the Post-Immigrant Era

Any attempt at describing the cultural world of the post-immigrant Jewish community of Montreal must proceed with caution. For one thing, the immigration process continues to bring new ethnic and cultural elements into the community and the cultural composition of the community is more fluid and complex than in the past. Countries of origin have changed drastically; since the late 1950s many North African Sephardim have augmented a declining Ashkenazi population, and more recently a smaller number of Israelis and Russians have taken up residence in the city. It is therefore premature to assess the social and cultural effect of this new amalgam, although it is important to note that a number of francophone authors of Sephardi background have made their appearance in recent years and won acclaim. So while a commentary on the post-World War II Jewish milieu is rendered difficult and must remain tentative, nonetheless a pattern of change and continuity has emerged that allows for some reasonable contentions.

Cultural departures from the past are immediately evident. English remains the primary *lingua franca* in the Montreal Jewish community and until recent years was almost the sole language of Jewish literary expression. Yiddish, despite the efforts of a number of dedicated devotees, diminished inexorably with the passing of the immigrant generation. Increasingly, only the elderly and the Chassidic segments of the community use the language as a vernacular, and even within these groups it is an open question whether future generations will be able to sustain the practice. Similarly, the introduction of courses in Yiddish at the university level, far from being signs of vitality, may be considered quite the reverse: academic study marks the end, not the beginning of a cultural process.

Still, the loss of the Yiddish "mother-tongue" is countered by many indications of continuity in communal affairs. Some of the major institutional agencies have adapted to the new circumstances while remaining loyal to the mandate that defined their origins. The Jewish Public Library, for example, continues to be a spirited centre of literary and intellectual activities, offering rich programs on Judaica and Jewish affairs, as well as topics of current social and political interest in English and French as well as in Yiddish. The Saidye Bronfman Centre functions as a showcase for artistic and theatrical presentations, including regular performances of Yiddish plays. On the political scene the former ideological ferment on behalf of working-class or radical causes has largely been replaced by a well-nigh unanimous espousal of pro-Israel support and an outspoken defence on behalf of civil rights issues and social tolerance. The once-divisive issues have been absorbed in a Jewish communal consensus that stresses unity over fractious differences.

One of the richest sources for understanding the social and cultural condition of the post-immigrant period resides in the stories and poems of the writers who witnessed the life of their time. The narratives of Jewish life in Montreal in the post-immigrant era were written by a large number of women and men determined to be writers. Much of this writing reveals a density of sociological observation even when the literary qualities are compromised by didacticism or apologetics; much of this writing will continue to have historical value despite these evident shortcomings. The most impressive versions of growing up Jewish are to be found in the writing of three major authors whose works comprise a virtual epic account of Jewish life in Montreal for over half a century: A.M. Klein, Irving Layton, and Mordecai Richler. In these writers we observe the artistic efforts of the children of immigrants whose source of creative energy was the conflicted biographical fact of their own dual identities. Their inner struggles to resolve the tension between the world of their mothers and fathers and the beckoning prospect of unencumbered individuality were transmuted into stirring imaginative texts of personal self-creation. And their stories of personal trial and affirmation became, in turn, the chronicle of the historic development of the community which had powerfully shaped their subjective beings.

Abraham Moses Klein (1909-1972) was the first distinctive Jewish voice in Canadian literature and the most influential Jewish writer of his generation. A lifelong Montrealer, he created a notable body of poetry, essays, and fiction from the complex cultural elements of his native city, and he fashioned memorable works of art out of his painful struggles with the contending cultural forces that exerted themselves on his consciousness.

For Klein, the formative element was the pious Chassidic family into which he was born and raised. From his parents he inherited a deep sentimental loyalty to their way of life which was structured in accordance with divine commandments and the holy calendar. In the traditional world of cheder, Talmud Torah, and synagogue, he studied the ancient texts of Judaism and discovered in the diction, grammar, and syntax of Tanach, Talmud, and Midrash an expressive vocabulary for his store of Jewish memory.

In his finest poems and stirring allegorical novel *The Second Scroll* (1951), Klein created richly-textured multilingual reflections on his own valiant attempt to incorporate ancient memory into modernist expression. He developed a unique lexicon—a brilliant melange of Yiddish and Hebrew terms, English renaissance diction recalling the King James Version of the Bible, and local French patois—to evoke the polyglot world of his Montreal. All of his writing conveyed his deep loyalty to the traditional pieties, but he set these evocations in disturbing autobiographical confessions of personal disbelief, transmuting his dilemma into a body of remarkable literature. In doing so he represented not only his personal crisis, but that faced by many of his contemporaries among the first-generation children of immigrants as they negotiated the stormy passage between the old and the new. More than any other modern Jewish writer, Klein summoned up a Judaic world which he regarded as precious and desirable, but admitted ruefully that the clarity and security it once exuded are no longer felt. His innumerable Judaic references recreate a world that lives in his imagination, but that traditional way of life materializes in his poems and fictions in the very act of disappearance, and he is compelled to acknowledge that he has moved beyond the bounds of its once sustaining authority.

Klein's importance for Montreal (and Canadian) Jewish letters derives from the powerful example of his life and work. At a time when Canadian literature was uncongenial to ethnic minorities, he dared make of Jewish Montreal—his foreign world with its obscure pre-modern customs and folklore—his true subject, and thus pioneered the way for younger writers who also sought to bridge the gap between immigrant origins and literary acceptance.

The second major voice of Jewish Montreal is that of Irving Layton whose writing career spans five decades and has produced over fifty volumes of poetry, fiction, essays, memoirs, literary criticism, and correspondence. In many ways, Layton's attitude to his Jewish heritage was influenced by his relationship with Klein, and particularly, his response to Klein's public role and its effect on his creative life. While only several years younger than Klein, Layton regarded him as a father-figure rather than contemporary, acknowledging his indebtedness to Klein's generous tutelage when he was just starting out. But the most significant lesson Layton took from the older, experienced writer did not concern poetic stylistics or idiom. It was the sad spectacle of Klein's demise, a closure Layton attributed to the older man's impossible attempt to wed his community role as public servant to his people—as publicist, editor, fund-raiser—and his private vocation as poet. The tension that afflicted Klein could not be resolved and ultimately resulted in silence. Layton's entire career was predicated on avoiding the self-destructive conflicts that stilled his mentor's final years.

The course of Layton's vocation reveals the kind of choices he made and the opportunities available to him. From the beginning he determined that his audience would not be confined to Jewish readers but to the literate public at large and his subject matter would not be limited to the parochial but embrace the universal. This willful determination to forge a new individual identity beyond religious or ethnic birthright marks Layton as a voice of his generation. The narrative of his life journey that emerges from his voluminous writings tells not only his personal story but that of his post-immigrant contemporaries as well—the foundation story of the modern Jewish intellectual. The details may vary but the over-arching story is typical: the ordeal of personal transformation, the elemental account of how Jewish children abandon the narrow, parochial world of their parents and community, for the open, exhilarating, domain of secular knowledge and worldly expansiveness. It locates the opening chapter in impoverished immigrant homes, traces the rupture from traditional belief, then continues with the espousal of radical political ideologies in the 1930s and 1940s, and concludes with the formulation of a cosmopolitan, humanistic credo to replace the out-moded particularism of ethnic origins.

But some decades later this version depicts the stages of political disillusionment suffered by the protagonist which results from a sombre reassessment of Democracy's failure to prevent the Holocaust and a belated awakening to the murderous reality of Stalinist communism. Again, Layton's responses synchronize with those of countless others. His odyssey as well as theirs moves toward closure in an open recognition of the centrality of Israel as the vital source of Jewish belonging in the post-immigrant world, and his avowal of a new-found belief in the Jewish national association.

This biographical trajectory of departure and return, of youthful aspirations and mature reconsideration, typified the core experience of many immigrant children in Montreal. And by placing it at the centre of his literary concerns, Layton gave permanent literary form to this transitory historical moment.

Mordecai Richler, one of Canada's leading novelists and one of the few Canadian writers to achieve an international reputation, has earned his literary prestige through a life-long dedication to his primary subject: remembering and reconstructing the Jewish enclave of his childhood in Montreal, or more particularly, his revered St. Urbain Street. Richler's art is that of a witness, the product of the very streets he commemorates, now committed to rendering the essential qualities of the place that formed him. "...I do feel forever rooted in St. Urbain Street," he said in his essay "The Uncertain World" (1969), "This was my time, my place, and I have elected myself to get it exactly right." His narratives, which meld memoir and fiction, resonate with a speaking voice that captures perfectly the regional diction, the remembered accents and syntax of his youth, providing the most exacting literary transcription of Jewish Montreal in Canadian fiction.

These versions have not been favourably received by many in the Jewish community. His mimetic rendering of the community's speech habits, cultural aspirations, and class distinctions, has caused some uneasiness among readers who see themselves mirrored in his comic distortions and satiric burlesques. Some have read these as clear evidence of the author's self-hatred, his frustrated attempt to strike against the inescapable bond of unhappy memory. But the psychological source of Richler's vision is less important (and finally unaccountable) than his use of these materials in imaginative art.

Richler was born in 1931 and came of age during the war years and their aftermath. His major fiction returns to those years, the matrix of his imagination. On the socio-economic level these fictions deal with the transformation of Jewish society in Montreal which saw the original immigrant neighbourhoods abandoned for the more affluent districts in the city's west end, and further still into the newly-constructed suburbs.

His attitude toward that unexceptional demographic change is best seen in the personae of his fictional characters. Typically his protagonist is a child of the old ghetto, haunted by the memory of the intense, vibrant life it once offered, but now removed from it by virtue of age and professional success. In his mind, past and present are juxtaposed, contrasting the energetic innocence of an impoverished childhood against the depleted ambitions and cultural incoherence of the recently enriched.

In his memorable character Duddy Kravitz, Richler achieves his fullest realization of his remembered Montreal at its most appealing and outrageous. While the novel in which he first appeared is a young man's work, the hero embodies all the contradictory qualities Richler saw at work in his generation—and which he shared. Here is the appetite, the ambition for success which would propel the children from immigrant homes into the surrounding hostile territory and claim recognition for individual merit and ability. The hero's boundless *chutzpa* acts to overcome the enmity of the dominanting host culture. He forces it to unmask its hypocritical polished manners as disguises for more rapacious appetites than he, in his innocence, had ever imagined or had the guile to cover up.

While Duddy's unconstrained energies are directed toward unscrupulous business deals and involve the exploitation of others, Richler nonetheless conceives of them as directed to a higher purpose than mere financial gain. Duddy's secret goal—pursuing his Zaide's injunction to purchase land because it is the source of human dignity—translates his crude materialism into spiritual quest. For Richler, the pathos of Duddy's contradictory actions, and by extension the actions of his contemporaries in the immigrant generation, lies not in his uncouth crassness and lack of refinement, but in his inability to distinguish between means and ends, his ignorance of moral law and its consequences. While the young protagonist loses his bearings in the unbridled chase after financial gain, it is the figure of the old-world immigrant Zaide who exemplifies the coveted spiritual ideal.

At the centre of Richler's fiction is social change and its corrosive effects on his familiar world. His satiric art, like that of satirists before him, is the expression of a conservative inclination measuring the thinness of contemporary life against the nostalgic recreations of memory. In his retrospective fiction he has foregrounded the parvenu, the uncouth kid from the slums who has scrambled to wealth but in his penthouse and limousine is still betrayed by bad manners and worse taste. Richler's chronicle of this emergent privileged class pronounces on their ineptitude and posturing, attributing their failure to the cultural and moral losses they incurred in the very process of gaining access to a world their immigrant parents could barely imagine.

The writings of Klein, Layton, and Richler encompass a half-century of Jewish life in Montreal. That extensive period saw the transformation of a Yiddish-speaking immigrant community into an integrated segment of the Montreal mosaic. These writers (along with many others of the same era) created a lasting literature by perceiving their personal ventures, enacted on Montreal's streets and neighbourhoods, as worthy materials for imaginative recreation. The result aptly reflects the condition of Jewish Montreal—in all its vitality and uncertainty, its achievements and inner conflicts. These writers witnessed the effect of the significant changes that transformed their traditional beginnings, just as they recorded the equally significant renewals and continuities that persist amidst change.

The Future of Montreal Jewry

The "Quiet Revolution" of the 1960s, which has utterly transformed Quebec society, did not exempt the Jewish community of Montreal from its effects. In its wake, it has brought about a major demographic shift as a significant portion of the Montreal Jewish community left Quebec, to be partially replaced with a new francophone Jewish immigration. The fact that the Montreal Jewish community, like many other ethnic communities in Quebec, historically opted for acculturation in the anglophone community, was likewise significant within a social, economic and cultural context in which francophone citizens of Quebec have asserted the cultural and economic powers to which they felt their preponderance in the population entitled them.

Revolutions, even quiet ones, have their victims. In this case, the Jewish community of Montreal has been confronted with the question of the sort of future it can look forward to. What that future will look like cannot now be discerned with any accuracy. One thing, however, appears clear. Whatever the future of Montreal Jewry will be will essentially depend upon the result of an ongoing debate in Quebec society. Will Quebec be a multicultural, multiethnic society which insists on conducting its official business in French or will it be a society which insists on the acculturation of "others" to its own norms? In other words, the debate initiated in Quebec by the presence of Jews for more than two centuries has been an ongoing one. A definitive conclusion to this debate is nowhere in sight.

Toward a History of Kashrut in Montreal

The Fight Over Municipal By-law 828 (1922-1924)

IRA ROBINSON

The Importance of Kashrut in Historical Analysis

IN THE JEWISH IMMIGRANT EXPERIENCE in North America in the late nineteenth and early twentieth centuries, much attention has been paid to what has been changed.[1] It was patently obvious to observers that much if not most of the Eastern European Jewish tradition was lost or discarded by Jews in the process of emigration and acculturation in North America. The question that has to be asked is "what remained"?[2] For the immigrant Jewish community of Montreal, this question was addressed by Israel Medres, a writer for the Montreal Yiddish daily, the *Keneder Odler*[3] in his memoir, *Tsvishn Tsvei Velt Milkhomes* (Between Two World Wars). Prior to the First World War, he wrote, orthodox Jews insisted on two things: the purchase of kosher meat and that their children learn a bit of Hebrew to be able to pray. The rest generally went by the boards.[4] The children's ability to pray, such as it was, manifested itself all too often on those occasions when departed relatives were formally remembered in the synagogue. Of this phenomenon Rabbi Yudel Rosenberg, a Montreal rabbi who plays an important role in this essay,[5] wrote to his son, Mayer Joshua:

> With regard to ...the laws of mourning, know, my son, that in these [North American] lands the rabbi has to be very expert in these laws, for the community members fear only the dead, and observe these commandments very punctiliously.[6]

The other major continuity noted by Medres was kosher meat. The insistence of the Jewish immigrants, regardless of their level of observance of the laws and customs of rabbinic Judaism in other areas, to purchase and consume meat certified as ritually "kosher" (proper) created a vast industry in all North American centers of Jewish life.[7] This industry was a source of income, power and prestige, for hundreds of people, and especially for immigrant Orthodox rabbis who usually had no other viable way to make a decent living or of exerting their influence in a community which, in most other instances, tended to regard them as basically irrelevant figures.

Despite the importance of *kashrut* as a factor in American Jewish history, it has not hitherto received that much scholarly attention.[8] This essay is designed to shed further light upon this subject.[9] It will further examine, in the context of *kashrut*, the Montreal Jewish community's interaction with the Montreal municipality at a formative stage in its development.

The Process of Passing By-Law 828

On June 5, 1922, Rabbi Yudel Rosenberg sent a letter to the Mayor of Montreal, Mederic Martin, urging him to introduce a by-law in Montreal, similar to one recently adopted in Toronto. It would govern the operation and sanitation of chicken killing establishments, "which would then be kept in a sanitary condition and would be directly under the control of our Rabbis and their representatives." Martin was asked to bring this matter before the City Council and the Executive Committee.[10]

Who was Rosenberg? If you read his letterhead, you would be informed that he was the "Chief Rabbi of the United Hebrew Orthodox Congregations of Montreal, Canada." What did that really mean? In America, after all, one often became chief rabbi through the aegis of the printer and the signmaker.[11] Rosenberg originally came to Montreal, in early 1919, because of opposition to Rabbi Hirsh Cohen's control of kosher slaughtering (*shehita*) in the city. The opposition group needed a rabbi for purposes of legitimation and they invited Rosenberg. From 1919-1921, Rosenberg and Cohen and their respective supporters fought each other for control of kosher meat in

Montreal. Finally, they found they couldn't beat each other so they joined in a joint *kashrut* directory and ultimately, with Rabbis Zalmanowitz and Garber, set themselves up as a local board of rabbis, "*di hige shtot rabbonim*"—The Rabbis of the City. Together they began opposing the pretentions to kashrut supervision of a new rabbi in Montreal, Joshua Hirschorn. This rabbinic cooperation was one important factor which would ultimately make possible the founding of the Montreal Jewish Community Council—the *Vaad Ha-Ir*—in late 1922.[12]

On June 6, 1922, the day after Rosenberg had written, Mayor Martin referred Rosenberg's letter to the City Council, which, on a motion by Alderman Lyon W. Jacobs, representing the St. Louis Ward and seconded by Alderman Rubenstein, referred the matter to the Executive Committee and to its Committee on Health.[13] It is worth noting that this initiative was doubtless considered a "Jewish" measure, being both moved and seconded by the two Jewish aldermen on Council.

The Council's Committee on Health invited Rosenberg to make a presentation at its next meeting, on June 30, when the subject of the proposed by-law would be taken up.[14]

Rosenberg, though he has been in Canada for nearly a decade at this time, was fluent in neither official language[15] and so he submitted a written statement in English instead, dated June 29, 1922.[16] It deserves to be cited in full:

> As I am not a fluent English speaker, I must present my request with my pen as a substitute for my voice to the board of Health.
>
> I beg that you take into consideration that Montreal should, in the Hygienic respect regarding chicken killing, not be lower than all large cities in Canada. Having been Chief Rabbi of Toronto for five years, it was there established a By-Law that poultry must not be killed in private places; not in a chicken store and not in a market, but there were established five special sanitary places where the Jewish rabbis thus occupied should kill the poultry under the supervision of the Chief Rabbi.

The same was also put in force in all other large Canadian cities; except Montreal which is still lacking in that respect like an Indian city in the middle ages.

I beg, educated gentlemen, that you consider that very many diseases which exist by [sic] people, also exist in poultry. In that I am well acquainted, for the Jewish people, upon discovering that a chicken is not all well inside, bring such chicken to me for examination to state if said chicken should be used as food. I find, from experience, that chickens suffer from the following diseases;—different smallpox in the intestines and belly and on the liver, consumption with ether in the lungs, water in the belly (Ascites), Cancer (Carcinoma), and other swelling diseases which are contagious to people.

Then, that myriads of flies make their residence on the blood of the chickens in the chicken stores and markets where the poultry is killed, the same flies poison the water which the live chickens drink; the same flies poison all kinds of foods which are to be found in the markets. How, I ask you learned gentlemen, can such a grave injustice be permitted in Montreal?

The Rabbis that kill the chickens are stationed all day in small, dark and filthy, unsanitary places with the result that not one becomes consumptive of their work. All this influenced me long ago that I request Dr. Boucher [director of the city's Board of Health] to do something about this, but without success, I regret. To-day, I again beg the Board of Health not to neglect this very necessary reform.

It should be ascertained an amount of sanitary places for killing poultry similar to the system now reigning in Toronto; where the Rabbis of chicken killing should kill the chickens according to the Jewish Religion under the supervision of the Chief Rabbis. I think that six such places will be sufficient for Montreal:

No I In district of St. Lawrence Market.

No II In district of Rachel's Market.

No III In Ontario Street.

No IV In Roy.
No V In Miland [sic, i.e. Mile End]
No VI In Papineau.

The government, if she does not desire, need not invest any money in this. It is very important that a By-Law be passed about this which should not later than in two months pass into existence.

With hopes that you will consider my ideas and fulfill my request which is also the earnest request of the entire Montreal Jewish population. I thank you in anticipation.

Rabbi Yodel Rosenberg

City Council did not act with the speed that Rosenberg requested. The process of making the By-Law "Concerning Poultry, Game and Fish" into law took not two months, as Rosenberg had hoped, but fully a year. The draft, which had been prepared in 1922, was delayed largely because of various objections which had been raised to draft versions of article 29, which limited the number of Jewish poultry slaughtering establishments to eight.[17] That article, written by Alderman Jacobs after consultation with a "high dignitary of the Hebrew religion",[18] probably Rabbi Hirsh Cohen, ultimately read:

> Not more than eight Jewish establishments for the slaughtering of poultry, exclusive of those situated in public markets, shall be allowed in the City, and no such establishments shall be opened and operated unless a permit to that effect be previously obtained from the city...
>
> The number of other slaughtering establishments shall not be limited, providing that the persons, firms, corporations or companies keeping the same conform, in every respect, to the provisions of this By-Law.[19]

The By-Law, number 828, was adopted by the Executive Committee on May 31, 1923 and by the Council on August 13.[20]

The Battle is Joined

Immediately after this By-Law was passed, Rabbi Cohen and the *Vaad Ha-Ir* were busy lobbying to make sure that the permits for poultry abattoirs would not be given save under their control. Thus in a letter of August 14, the executive secretary of the *Vaad*, William Nadler, recounted a meeting held between Rabbi Cohen, representing the Rabbinical Committee of the Jewish Community Council, Alderman Jacobs and Dr. Boucher requesting that no permit be given for the establishment of a Jewish chicken abattoir "unless and until he shall have first been recommended in writing for this permit by Rabbi Cohen or the Montreal Council of Orthodox rabbis" in order to "enable...the Montreal Council of Orthodox Rabbis to control the slaughtering of fowl by authorized persons, and in accordance with the Jewish Dietary Laws."[21]

What were the implications of this control? If the *Vaad Ha-Ir* was to fulfill its mandate to control the *kashrut* system in Montreal, it was, of course, necessary to make sure that there were no "independents" working outside its aegis. Thus, on August 17, eight requests for permits were received from people connected with the *Vaad Ha-Ir*. The applicants, who included Rabbis Cohen, Dubitzsky and Zalmanowitz, proposed to establish the slaughterhouses at 1040 St. Lawrence, 25 Roy E., St. Lawrence near Mozart, City Hall near Mt. Royal, St. Lawrence, between St. Viateur and St. Bernard, 33 Ontario E., Pine Ave., between St. Dominique and Colonial and 1527 Marquette.[22]

On August 29, Alderman A.D. Tessier, representing the Papineau district, who had objected to this procedure, withdrew his objections provided that one of those permits be issued to the Papineau Jewish community through him. The *Vaad* agreed to this compromise and in a letter dated August 30, requested that the other seven permits should be granted directly to them as a corporate body instead of to the individuals.[23]

There was more to these requests than was immediately apparent, however. Rabbi Cohen and his supporters were so active so quickly because the authority of the *Vaad Ha-Ir* was being seriously challenged at this time by the secession of Rabbis Rosenberg and Hirschorn and seven slaughterers in January of 1923.[24] A new Kosher Meat War had commenced which would last until 1925. It was a struggle which would seriously test the staying power of the *Vaad*. In this context, it was imperative for Rabbi Cohen and his allies to lock up the places and freeze out Rosenberg's slaughterers and thus enhance their own legitimacy.

Rosenberg's protest was not long in coming. As reported in the *Montreal Gazette* of September 9, Rosenberg and Hirschorn wrote Mayor Martin that the Jewish Community Council was not in fact representative of the Jewish Community as a whole, that several Jewish organizations which were listed as favoring the proposal were in fact against it, that fully 75% of the Jewish population of Montreal was opposed to the measure and that the By-Law should be withdrawn, "allowing all who keep sanitary places to kill poultry."[25]

On September 16, the *Keneder Odler*, which had spawned the *Vaad Ha-Ir* and which editorially supported Rabbi Cohen and the *Vaad* to the hilt, reacted to Rosenberg's protest. It accused Rosenberg of inventing the names of non-existent synagogues to support the cause of the "renegades" *(farreter)* as the *Keneder Odler* invariably called them. As the article stated:

> The renegades, who have sought to destroy all that is holy and dear to Montreal Jews seek now to also help the chicken dealers in [their] struggle against order. The former rabbis Yudel Rosenberg and Hirschorn have sent to the city Mayor a protest against the decision that the eight [slaughter] rooms be under the control of the *Vaad Ha-Ir*...
>
> It is interesting that in Yudel Rosenberg and Hirschorn's protest they say that they represent three quarters of Montreal Jewry. This was between Rosh ha Shana and Yom Kippur, when ordinary flesh and blood people guard themselves from telling a lie. However it seems that former rabbis are not plain flesh and blood people and what others cannot do they may.[26]

The next day, September 17, the *Vaad* made its formal response to the charges in a letter to Mayor Martin. In it they reasserted that they represented "over 90% of all the Hebrew Synagogues, Benevolent Societies, Loan Syndicates and Labor Organizations in Montreal" and branded as false the claim that 75% of the community opposed them. They decried as equally false the charge that they were attempting to create a monopoly. As they stated, somewhat disingenuously, "the Jewish Community rabbis you will admit know what is in the best religious interests of the Jewish community."

The *Vaad*'s letter further asserted that, contrary to Rosenberg's accusation, the organizations named on their letterhead had in fact participated in the organization while "the largest and most important Jewish Congregations, Benevolent Societies, Loan Syndicates and Labor Organizations are loyal supporters of the Montreal Jewish Community Council," and the "Canadian Jewish Eagle and the Canadian Jewish Chronicle, which constitutes [sic] the Jewish Press of this Province are the champions of the Montreal Jewish Community Council." The letter concluded with a request for a meeting with the mayor. The letter was subsequently given to the press, and it appeared in the Gazette of September 18 with the interesting addition that Rabbis Rosenberg and Hirschorn were characterized, as in the *Keneder Odler* article, as "ex-Rabbis."[27]

The leaders of the *Vaad* met with Mayor Martin on September 20 and there was possibly a second meeting held on September 26.[28] For the moment, the *Vaad* had seemingly triumphed, but not for long. Its opponents had one more recourse—the legal system.

Indeed the *Keneder Odler* article reacting to Rosenberg's protest had surmised as much:

> Lately they [Rosenberg et al] have been seeking through the courts to coerce butchers away from the *Vaad Ha-Ir*...The renegades have brought the matter into court. They wish to extract from a lawyer a *hekhsher* for their deeds, something they cannot extract from rabbis. However they truly will obtain from the lawyers the same hekhsher that they got from the rabbis.[29]

A suit was brought in Quebec Superior Court before Judge Louis Coderre against the City of Montreal by "Dame Hattie Vineberg of the City and District of Montreal, wife separate as to property of Julius Friedman, of the same place and the latter to authorize his wife for the purposes hereof, the said Dame Hattie Vineberg there carrying on business as poultry dealer under the name and style of J. Friedman and Co., and Leib Simon Woloz, of the same place, slaughterer and [of?] cattle and poultry."[30]

The suit argued that the provision of the By-Law limiting the amount of Jewish poultry slaughtering establishments while allowing all other such establishments was unconstitutional "particularly as creating class and religious distinctions to the prejudice of the Jewish citizens" and would result in "great and irreparable injury...insofar as it affects the trade and business of Jewish poultry dealers within the city of Montreal."

On April 11, 1924, Judge Coderre found for the plaintiffs, declared article 20 unconstitutional and awarded them court costs which amounted to $272.85. The City did not appeal and the by-law was suitably amended in May, 1924.[31]

What have we learned from the story of By-Law 828?

The first thing to note is that the attempt to use the political system to further the power of the rabbinate and the organized Jewish community failed on constitutional grounds, despite the relative receptiveness of the municipal government of Montreal in satisfying what it conceived of as a legitimate request by the Jewish community. This failure marked the limits of the use of the political system as a means of establishing and sustaining a monopoly of this sort. Secondly, the failure of the court to sustain article 29 of By-Law 828, indicated that in Montreal, as elsewhere in Canada and the United States, the rabbis could only hope to enforce or defend their rights through the civil court system rather than through legislated monopolies.

Finally, the end of the fight over By-Law 828 helps to explain the way in which the "Kosher Meat War" of 1923-25 ended. In the battle between the partisans of Rosenberg and Cohen, there had been a stalemate with the advantage rather on Cohen's side. In my opinion it was the Vineberg case, coupled with the decision in another Quebec

Superior Court Case (Getsel Laxer et al vs. Jewish Butchers Society of Montreal et al) on March 18, 1925 which similarly upheld the legal rights of Rosenberg's "renegades" against the *Vaad Ha-Ir*, ultimately brought about an end of the Kosher Meat War of 1922-1925 with a return to the status quo ante bellum.[32]

Notes

1.See Moses Rischin, *The Promised City,* New York: Harvard University Press, 1970 and Irving Howe, *World of Our Fathers,* New York: Harcourt Brace Jovanovich, 1976, for examples of this.

2.Jenna Joselit takes Rischin to task on this issue in her "What Happened to New York's' Jewish Jews': Moses Rischin's *The Promised City* Revisited," American Jewish History 73 (1983), 163-172.

3.See Zachary M. Baker, "Montreal of Yesterday: a Snapshot of Jewish Life in Montreal During the Era of Mass Immigration," Ira Robinson et al., eds., *An Everyday Miracle: Yiddish Culture in Montreal,* Montreal: Véhicule Press, 1990, 39-52.

4.Israel Medres, *Tsvishn Tsvei Velt Milkhomes* (Montreal, 1964), 32.

5.On Rosenberg, see Ira Robinson, "A Letter From the Sabbath Queen: Rabbi Yudel Rosenberg Addresses Montreal Jewry," Ira Robinson et al., eds., *An Everyday Miracle: Yiddish Culture in Montreal,* ibid. , 101-114; "The Uses of the Hasidic Story: Rabbi Yudel Rosenberg and His Tales of the Greiditzer Rabbi," *Journal of the Society of Rabbis in Academia* 1, nos. 1-2 (1990), 17-25; "Literary Forgery and Hasidic Judaism: the Case of Rabbi Yudel Rosenberg," *Judaism* 40 (1991), 61-78; "The Education of an American Orthodox Rabbi: Mayer Joshua Rosenberg Comes to Holyoke, Massachusetts," *Judaism* 40 (1991), 543-551. Cf. also Eli Yassif, ed. *The Golem of Prague and Other Tales of Wonder,* [Hebrew], Jerusalem: Mossad Bialik, 1991), introduction.

6.Robinson, "The Education," 549.

7.See Harold Gastwirt, *Fraud, Corruption and Holiness: the Controversy Over the Supervision of Jewish Dietary Practice in New York City, 1881-1940,* Port Washington, NY: Kennikat Press, 1974.

8.At best it seems to receive glancing, anecdotal attention in works devoted to a survey of the Orthodox Jewish community. Other than Gastwirt, cited above, there are no monographs devoted to this subject. An exceptional article is Moshe Stern, "Winnipeg Kashruth: a History," *The Nathan Lockshin Memorial Journal* (Winnipeg, 1982), 61-77.

9.Ira Robinson, "The Kosher Meat War and the Jewish Community

Council of Montreal, 1922-1925", *Canadian Ethnic Studies* 22, 2 (1990), 41-53.

10. Letter from Yudel Rosenberg to Mederic Martin, June 5, 1922. File on By-Law 828, Archives Municipales de Montréal, no. 13135 (AM).

11. On the famous incident in which a rabbi in New York ascribed his "chief rabbinate of the United States" to the sign painter, see *American Jewish Historical Society* (1954), p. 172, n. 128.

12. Robinson, "Kosher Meat War," 44-45

13. Note in file, AM.

14. Assistant City Clerk to Rosenberg, June 27, 1922. AM.

15. Rosenberg's statement of June 29, 1922 begins, "As I am not a fluent English speaker."

16. AM.

17. Lyon W. Jacobs to Jules Crepeau, May 2, 1923 and May 15, 1923. AM.

18. Commison de Santé report of July 12, 1923. AM.

19. "No. 828, printed text of the By-Law, 9.

20. Ibid, 1.

21. William Nadler to Jules Crepeau, August 14, 1923. AM

22. Letters to Dr. Boucher from Rabbi H. Cohen, A. Marcovich, Rabbi A. Zalmonovitch, S. Silver, Louis Solomon, Raphael Epstein, S. Lachavitsky and Rabbi S. Dubitzky, dated from August 17-20, 1923. AM.

23. Dr. A.D. Tessier to Jules Crepeau, August 29, 1923; Montreal Council of Orthodox Rabbis to Jules Crepeau, August 30, 1923. AM.

24. Robinson, "Kosher Meat War," 45ff.

25. "Rabbis Protest Against By-Law," *Montreal Gazette*, September 9, 1923.

26. "*Shulen mit Nemen fun der Haftora Helfen di Farreter in Kamf Gegen der Stodt*," *Keneder Odler*, September 16, 1923, 1.

27. Montreal Jewish Community Council to Mederic Martin, September 17, 1923. AM. Cf. "Letter to Mayor on Poultry By-Law," *Montreal Gazette*, September 18, 1923.

28. E. L'Espérance, Secretary to the Mayor, to William Nadler, September 18, 1923. Canadian Jewish Congress Archives, Jewish Community Council File.

29. *Keneder Odler*, September 16, 1923.

30. Superior Court, Province of Quebec, District of Montreal, no. 163. AM.

31. Guillaume St. Pierre to President and Members of the Executive

Council, May 1, 1924. AM.

32. Robinson, "Kosher Meat War," 48-49. Cf. Superior Court, Province of Quebec, District of Montreal, no. 3312. Archives du Ministère de Justice, Province de Québec.

The Politics of Dialogue
Rapprochement Efforts Between Jews and French Canadians: 1939-1960

JACK JEDWAB

ONE OF THE PRINCIPAL FEATURES of the historic dialogue between the leadership of Montreal's Jewish and French Canadian communities was the political dimension which was often present during the exchange. One of the pioneers of Jewish-French Canadian *rapprochement*, Jacques Langlais, recently observed that many who were once involved in Catholic action and ultimately led *rapprochement* initiatives "found themselves on the political scene during the last few decades and at the present time."[1] Under these circumstances, it is not surprising that the Jewish community's political spokesgroup, the Canadian Jewish Congress, has traditionally played a vital role in the pursuit of initiatives aimed at better understanding between Jews and French Canadians. As there were frequent strains between the two communities, those leaders involved in dialogue were regularly confronted with a certain degree of political risk within their own respective constituencies. Still, whether their constituents approved or disapproved of such discussion of which they were often unaware, there almost always existed some channel of communication.

With the Quiet Revolution of the 1960s and the introduction of Vatican II, it appeared as though numerous obstacles to dialogue between Jews and Catholics were removed. Contact between members of different communities in an increasingly multiethnic context rose considerably. But with the relative secularisation of Quebec society during that decade, dialogue between ethnic groups eventually came to dominate if not displace the interreligious dialogue which had once prevailed. Moreover, in large measure the government supplanted the clergy as the major "broker" in the resolution of intergroup tensions.

In the study of Jewish and French Canadian relations, much attention has been directed to the period from the beginning of the twentieth century through the Second World War, when the Montreal Jewish community confronted a heightened degree of anti-Semitism. There has been important divergence in the approach taken by analysts who have evaluated the historic relationship between Jews and French Canadians during this period. While some have stressed the incompatibility of the French Canadian and Jewish religions and/or cultures, others have emphasized the two communities' common struggle for cultural survival over the past two centuries. One observer has described as a missed rendez-vous the failure for the two groups to achieve a successful dialogue before the Second World War.[2]

Beginning in the mid-1940s, Jews throughout North America experienced significant change in their relationship with the broader society and in particular, with the Christian community. In his book *World of Our Fathers*, Irving Howe points out that as the word Holocaust reached the American people, anti-Semitism ceased to be respectable, and he adds that, for nearly two decades, Jews "breathed easier."[3] According to scholars David Rome and Jacques Langlais, both in Quebec and the rest of Canada, English and French Canadians alike were re-examining both attitude and behaviour towards the Jewish community. As a consequence of this, while anti-Semitism was still persistent, there was a substantial decline in the public expression of stereotypes directed at the Jewish community.[4]

In this article, we will look at the evolving relationship between Jewish and French Canadians from the post-war period to the end of the 1950s. Particular attention will be paid to the leadership which emerged in the two communities to spearhead rapprochement initiatives. The creation in the 1950s of the Jewish-French Canadian dialogue group known as the Cercle Juif de Langue Française and the role of the Canadian Jewish Congress will be highlighted. As we shall observe, certain French Canadians who in the pre-war period represented a major obstacle to dialogue, ultimately made a vital contribution to rapprochement with the Montreal Jewish community in the decade before the Quiet Revolution.

It is difficult to fully understand the changing relationship between Jews and French Canadians without examining the two communities position vis-à-vis Montreal's English Protestant community. From the beginning of the twentieth century, the insularity of the French Catholic community, combined with the English Protestant minority's desire to maintain strict control over its institutions, resulted in the Montreal Jewish community assuming perhaps greater responsibility for it own social and institutional development than was the case elsewhere in Canada and the United States. As Quebec's education and charitable systems were divided along confessional and linguistic lines, social interaction between French Catholics, Anglo-Protestants and Jews was somewhat more infrequent in Montreal than elsewhere in North America. As the other groups created their own hospitals, golf clubs and summer camps, so too did the Montreal Jewish community. With the relative failure of either the Anglo-Protestants or French Canadians to display what as been described as "an attitude of receptivity" some suggested that the Montreal Jewish community constituted a "third solitude." Yet others have referred to the Montreal Jewish community as a "world between." [5]

Leadership in the Jewish community felt troubled by the impact the English-French conflict would have on its rapprochement initiatives. Some believed that this was in part a source of the problems which existed between Jews and French Canadians. While it would be too simplistic to confine the problem between Jews and French Canadians to this situation, it certainly aggravated existing tensions between the two communities. There was a perception which existed amongst some French Canadians that the Jews were "on the side of the English." There were few illusions about the potential for playing a role in resolving the historically rooted tension between the two groups. Many community leaders would have concurred with certain observers of this dispute concerning the "...externally correct but cold and formal nature of the public relations between the two groups—more like those of diplomatic relations between two foreign states than between two "racial" elements in the same state".[6]

Anti-Semitism

Both in United States and Canada, levels of anti-Semitism reached alarming heights in the 1930s and 1940s.[7] Some areas of North America were more influenced than others by such sentiment. With its large French Catholic majority, the province of Quebec was clearly affected by this phenomenon in a unique way relative to other parts of the continent. A disproportionate number of Quebec intellectuals, it would seem, transmitted anti-Semitic views to the population. Moreover, with their relatively higher degree of isolation, many French Canadians appeared more susceptible to being exploited by authoritarian ideologues. During the Great Depression, an increasingly important segment of the province's clerically based intellectual elite, was influenced by corporatist and fascist ideologies and some were actively engaged in the promotion of such doctrines.

One of the more influential French Canadian clerics of the period, Abbé Lionel Groulx, engaged in the dissemination of anti-Semitic propaganda through such publications as *L'Action Française* and *L'Action Nationale Catholique*.[8] In perhaps the most important review of Quebec history, Groulx's "traditionalist" expression of nationalism is described as incorporating other characteristic right-wing themes of the 1930s. Apart from admiration for fascism, anti-Semitism was fairly widespread. Many people saw Jewish merchants, financiers, trade unionists and intellectuals as a threat and some even regarded them as agents of a vast international plot against the nation and the Catholic religion. Such ideas were able to reach a wider audience when, in the mid-1930s and through much of the forties, the newspaper *Le Devoir*, then under the editorship of Georges Pelletier, heavily indulged in the spread of anti-Semitism.[9] Calls for such measures as expulsion or systematic discrimination of Jews were generally confined to groups on the far right, such as Adrian Arcand and his group of Nazi followers who published "le Fasciste Canadien" between 1935 and 1938.[10]

Officials of Jewish organizations, associated with the Canadian Jewish Congress, monitored the activity of these publications. Repeated warnings were issued to those newspapermen deemed to be responsible for promoting anti-Jewish views. During the mid-1930s, Canadian Jewish Congress Executive Director, H.M. Caiserman, communicated with francophone media, considered both favourable and unfavourable to the Jewish population, and called upon them to stem the growth of anti-semitism.[11] In Quebec, the Catholic Church was considered the ultimate arbitrator in conflicts between Jewish and French Canadians. Leadership of the Jewish community believed that clerical intervention was essential to stem the rise of anti-Semitism in the 1930s. In this regard, CJC officials considered it important to "...sonder les positions de la hiérarchie catholique, et surtout de mesurer jusqu'à quel point il pourrait être possible de rallier le haut clergé à la lutte que comptait entreprendre le CJC..."[12] But Canadian Jewish Congress outreach to certain francophone opinion leaders of the period generally confronted indifference to community concerns over anti-Semitism.[13]

Political Ties

During the 1930s, while dialogue with the Catholic hierarchy proved largely unsuccessful in combatting anti-Semitism, some progress in pursuit of the latter objective was achieved on the political front. During elections held from 1916 to 1936, the Quebec Jewish community regularly maintained a representative in the provincial Liberal government. During the mandates of Premiers Lomer Gouin and Alexandre Taschereau, with certain exceptions, the Montreal Jewish community appeared to enjoy relatively good cooperation from provincial authorities and possessed an avenue with which to put forth some of its principal concerns. This was demonstrated by Premier Taschereau in his efforts to accommodate the community with the creation of a separate Jewish school board.[14] While the Liberals showed greater sensitivity to community concerns, it appeared by contrast that a segment of the provincial Conservatives were unsympathetic to the community and were at times prepared to exploit anti-Jewish sentiment. In spite of the perception that certain provincial Conservatives were willing to incite prejudice against the Jewish people, in a 1938 by-election in the largely Jewish riding of St. Louis, Louis Fitch became the first Jewish Conservative/Union Nationale candidate elected to the provincial Legislature. With significant support from the more recently arrived Jewish immigrants, the ardent Zionist Fitch was part of a political party with an important nationalist component.[15]

Fitch was by no means elected as a result of his constituents' support for the platform of the Union Nationale then, led by Premier Maurice Duplessis, but rather due to the weakness of his Liberal opponent, labour leader Raoul Trépanier. In its assessment of the by-election victory, the local Jewish press concluded that:

> The state of Utopia when a man's racial and religious label will be of no consequence has unhappily not yet been reached and we cannot forget that politics in the country have distinct racial colouring. Under such circumstances, the Jews could ill-afford to throw prudence to the winds and sacrifice a riding which has long had a Jewish representative.[16]

Fitch was confident in his ability to have an impact on opinions held by French Canadians with respect to the Jewish community. With his exceptional command of the French language, during his brief tenure in the Quebec Legislative Assembly, Fitch made the following appeal:

> Des maintes côtés, les ambitions, les voeux et les idéaux les plus chéris de la race juive touchent au rêve immortel de la race canadienne-française. Comme vous, nous avons derrière nous une histoire dont les pages débordent de dévouement, de luttes et de sacrifices évoqués par l'amour indestructible de notre tradition, de notre culture, de notre foi.

Fitch reported to the Quebec Legislature on the activities of Adrien Arcand and the spread of anti-Semitism in the province. He called upon the government to take steps to curb their vile attacks. Following Fitch's intervention, Premier Duplessis rose to publicly dissociate his party from such reprehensible doctrines.[17]

Community Relations and the Conscription Crisis

Within a year of his by-election victory, Fitch was defeated in the 1939 general election. At that time, Conservative/Union Nationale leader Maurice Duplessis waged his electoral campaign on opposition to Canada's participation in World War II. The victory of the provincial Liberals under Adélard Godbout was primarily the result of his perceived ability to convince the federal Liberals not to impose compulsory military service. The majority of French Canadians counted on a promise from then federal Liberal Prime Minister Mackenzie King not to introduce conscription.[18]

The already strained relations between Jews and French Canadians suffered further as a consequence of the latter group's staunch opposition to participation in the war effort. This resulted in inevitable conflict with the Jewish community which was unequivocal in its support for the maximal initiative to be deployed by the Canadian population. Relations once again deteriorated when in 1942 a plebiscite was called to reconsider the promise made by Prime Minister Mackenzie King not to impose conscription for military service. In its pro-conscription stand, Canadian Jewish Congress urged Canadians to stand on guard for the country and Jews to fight the totalitarian menace abroad.[19] In his column in the *Canadian Jewish Chronicle*, A.M. Klein described the anti-conscriptionists' claim to be for the defense of Canada as a "pretence and a sorry spectacle to behold." While confident of a victory in the plebiscite, Klein felt that it was critical for an overwhelming majority to support conscription so as not to allow fascists to exploit divisions in the population. He concluded that:

> It devolves therefore upon every citizen... to add his ballot to the affirmative avalanche which must ensue on the 27th; and in that decision Canadian Jewry must play the part which both its Canadianism and its Judaism demand![20]

Among the more prominent organizers of the anti-conscription campaign were Gérard Fillion and André Laurendeau, both of whom would emerge as influential figures in post-war Quebec. The French

Canadian opposition to conscription organized its campaign around a political movement, known as La Ligue pour la Défense du Canada which ultimately evolved into a political party known as the Bloc Populaire. The demonstrations organized by the Bloc Populaire against conscription often served as rallying points for anti-Semites.[21]

In his memoirs, Laurendeau recalled that at a youth rally to protest against conscription in March 1942, following several speeches, cries of "Down with international finance!" and "Down with the Jews" deteriorated into outbreaks of violence as "little gang[s]" smashed windows in Jewish shops. In his memoirs published two decades later, Laurendeau expressed his astonishment at such behaviour. He suspected that disciples of the Brown shirts of Quebec Nazi leader Adrian Arcand were responsible for these incidents. Those times, he observed, were tainted by anti-Semitism which, he added, was an ideology that did not guide the views put forth by the Bloc Populaire.[22] He concluded however that the crowds which appeared at the rallies had perhaps inherited the vague anti-Semitism of the Depression which he referred to as influenced by "pseudo-religious emotion." Although they expressed it more noisily than others, he contended that French Canadians had no monopoly on this prejudice. According to Laurendeau "this sentiment was older than Nazism and had no connection with dogmatic racism". More often than not, he added, "...it was a skin deep sentiment, unpleasant enough, but luckily quite harmless." The future editor of *Le Devoir* concluded that:

> In the end, Canadian Jews, through their national organization, declared themselves officially in favour of Yes in the plebiscite. That was certainly no surprise! Nor were we much surprised to see this stand cause a mild stir in the anti-conscriptionist camp.[23]

A former disciple of Lionel Groulx, on many occasions during the post war period Laurendeau eloquently recanted the anti-Semitism of his youth. Still, in his reflections on the conscription crisis, Laurendeau's assessment is symptomatic of the difficulty, during the post-war period, for certain prominent French Canadian leaders to come to terms with the experience of the 1930s and the war years. He was not alone in this regard. In reviewing a book on the history of French Canada, Pierre Elliot Trudeau complained that the author unduly brought out the anti-Semitism of the 1930s, which, he argued, was actually quite restrained. The perception that the manifestations of anti-Semitism in the thirties and forties were "relatively harmless" is indicative of a failure to understand the total consequence of such behaviour at that time, and the potential impact on its victims.[24] The by-product of this anti-Semitism was expressed in countless ways. The resistance to Jewish immigration was but one of the outcomes of domestic anti-Semitism throughout the continent. Surveys conducted in the immediate postwar period indicate that a majority of Canadians remained opposed to European immigration. In Quebec, anti-immigration sentiment was felt somewhat more strongly than in the rest of Canada. When in opposition, the Union Nationale and its leader, Maurice Duplessis, exploited French Canadian fears about the potential arrival of large numbers of Jewish immigrants. In November 1943, Duplessis claimed to have discovered evidence proving that a deal was in preparation to assure Jewish financing of the next provincial Liberal campaign in exchange for the establishment of 100,000 Jewish refugees on the farms of the province. It was a preposterous allegation based on a forgery that had been sent to Duplessis.[25]

Just prior to the end of the war, a vehement expression of resistance to Jewish immigration was exemplified by the actions of the Société Saint-Jean-Baptiste (SSJB). As Co-President of the SSJB in 1944, a twenty-seven year old Roger Duhamel led the organization in a campaign against immigration. Bringing some thirty organizations together, the SSJB developed a plan against massive immigration. The organization contended that imperialist and leftist groups were insisting on the admission of large numbers of refugees. The participation of the SSJB in this campaign was co-ordinated by Jean Drapeau (later mayor of Montreal) who, by the spring of 1944, had obtained over 150,000 signatures for a petition opposing immigration. According to officials of the organization, the ethnic origin of these refugees was no secret. The SSJB leadership suggested that:

> Des filiales du Canadian Jewish Congress organisent leur réception et leur répartition. L'organisation juive, au Canada, est de plus en plus complète. La Hebrew Free Loan Association donne une grande expansion à son "Prêt d'honneur, pour les étudiants juifs nésséciteux et pour les artisans désirant s'établir à leur compte". Avant longtemps, les réfugiés, bénéficiaires d'un Prêt d'honneur, commanderont, dans leurs entreprises, à des employés canadiens-français.[26]

In the post-war period, Drapeau, Duhamel, Fillion and Laurendeau all emerged in important leadership roles where they had occasion to interact with the Montreal Jewish community and participated (actively) in Jewish-French Canadian dialogue. Indeed, by the 1950's, their newspapers, *Le Devoir* and *La Patrie* were regularly denouncing anti-Semitism and encouraging the establishment of ties with the Montreal Jewish community.

One of the postwar pioneers of rapprochement between Montreal Jews and French Canadians was *Canadian Jewish Chronicle* editor A.M. Klein (who eventually emerged as one of the most celebrated literary figures in the Jewish community). Like the aforementioned French Canadian opinion makers, Klein employed his writing talents to promote better understanding between the two groups. Despite his frequent denunciations of anti-Semitic activity in Quebec, by 1944 A.M. Klein was concerned that various respectable publications, emanating from the other Canadian provinces and the United States had, on the question of racism, "gone to town" on the province of Quebec. Klein questioned the motives for these incessant attacks on the entire French Canadian population. He reiterated the view that there were forces which sought to exploit race hatred and religious bigotry in the province and regarded as crucial the need to "unmask the perpetrators of such hatred." Still, he objected to editorial writers going out of their way to suggest that the entire province was a bastion of intolerance and that all that was "French-speaking" carried the anti-Semitic virus. Klein insisted that this was simply untrue and one had a right to question the motives of those engaged in such wholesale prosecution. He described the views inspiring many of the sweeping criticisms levelled at Quebec, in the following terms:

> ...the pious defense of a discriminated minority is being used as an instrument of denigration against the French-Canadian minority, or the crusader, adopting the tactic of stop, thief, is pointing to Quebec anti-Semitism only to draw attention off his own. In some cases, both objectives are sought.[27]

The Canadian Jewish Congress and the French Catholic Clergy

When the Union Nationale returned to power in 1944 the Quebec episcopate differed significantly from that which existed in 1939. It was clear that during the war there was a reduction in the influence of French Catholic leadership. Quebec politicians seemed able to exert greater authority over the clergy throughout much of the province. Generally successful in his disputes with clerical leaders, Union Nationale Premier Maurice Duplessis once remarked that "the Bishops 'ate' out of his hands."[28]

At the very beginning of the 1940s, responsibility for the Montreal archdiocese was assumed by Monseigneur Joseph Charbonneau. Papal authorities in Rome and civil authorities in Canada were at least informally consulted over the appointment. According to one analyst, in the desperate mood of the 1940s, the papacy in Rome was not interested in another right-wing nationalist and ultra-conservative prelate in Canada's largest city.[29]

Born in Ontario, Monseigneur Charbonneau was considered to be neither a French Canadian nationalist, nor a Catholic exclusivist. He declared his intention to be the Archbishop of all Montrealers and not merely of the Roman Catholics of the city. Indeed, he was widely regarded as an outspoken liberal and a supporter of pluralism. Among other things, he believed in Canadian unity, in a materially reduced role for the Church and in a larger social role for the state. Monseigneur Charbonneau was perceived to be the "people's" Archbishop, and was considered a champion of the impoverished and the working class.[30]

In the immediate post-war period, the Montreal Jewish community leadership reactivated its Public Relations Committee with a particular emphasis on building ties with the French Canadian population. It did so primarily through contact with the clerical leadership. Despite the existence of a formal Christian-Jewish dialogue, the process initiated by Canadian Jewish Congress in the late 1940s had a limited focus on theological discussion. Led by Saul Hayes and David Rome, the Canadian Jewish Congress moved quickly to enhance ties with the French Catholic hierarchy. The programme was largely directed by David Rome who regularly reported on developments in the Catholic Church as they potentially impacted on the Jewish community. Rome described the most valuable work of the Committee as the establishment of contacts with elements of the French-Canadian population that "shape[d] its thinking."[31] The Canadian Jewish Congress attempted to reach the most accessible and interested members of the Catholic Church through the Montreal Archdiocese.

In January, 1946, the Joint Public Relations Committee of Canadian Jewish Congress and B'nai Brith established a sub-committee on French Public Relations aimed at improving ties between Jews and French Canadians. Indeed, the January, 1946 programme envisaged that:

> ...the Church can be a valuable ally of the Joint Public Relations Committee in its work. The Church had recognized the duty it has to educate it adherents and the failure it had made of the job to date.[32]

According to a Canadian Jewish Congress report, many of the leading clergymen were eager for the Church to pursue democratic action and repel fascist doctrine. There was a recognition that it would be difficult to reach the millions in the Church and therefore, the support of lay and clerical leadership would be solicited. It was hoped that the message could be then transmitted through synods, assemblies and conferences. The programme was pursued in cooperation with the Canadian Council of Christians and Jews and the Roman Catholic Church in Canada.

CJC officials hoped to enlist the support of the clergy in their campaign against anti-Semitism. Some observed a distinct change in the attitude of French Catholics towards Jews following World War II.

Whenever the pre-war period was recalled, French Canada was perceived to have been a "hot-bed of anti-Jewish feeling in Canada." By the fifties, according to CJC officials, anti-Semitism was no worse in Quebec than elsewhere in Canada.[33] There was a degree of uncertainty concerning the motivation for the partial change in attitude amongst French Canadians. While some attributed it to a Catholic policy aimed at conversion, others suggested it was linked to a more generalized concern to prevent atheism from spreading to the population. Whatever the rationale, from the standpoint of the Jewish community leadership it was subordinate to the need to maintain cordial relations with French Catholics who constituted a large part of the Canadian population.

In the late 1940s, Archbishop Charbonneau received representatives of Canadian Jewish Congress for a lengthy discussion of various questions of interest to Jews. Charbonneau reaffirmed his contempt for anti-Semitism and all other forms of racial expression and claimed he had acted against it whenever it had presented itself. During "the terrible days" of Arcand, he ensured that action was taken against the Nazi publication *Le Goglu*. A special committee created by the Archbishop to deal with Jewish questions—the Comité Saint-Paul—played an important role in combatting anti-Semitism in the post-war period. The Archbishop's Comité St. Paul played an instrumental role in the suppression of *Le Goglu*.[34] The newspaper had been banned by the government early in the war as a subversive publication, but with the post-war repeat of these regulations, the publication re-emerged as viciously anti-Semitic as previously. The Comité St. Paul urged the editor to suspend publication. The editor refused to accept this demand and proceeded to attack the clerical leadership for its "pro-Jewish policies." In spite of its resistance, the publication of *Le Goglu* was indeed suspended and did not reappear in any other guise.[35]

On yet another occasion, the Catholic clergy's denunciation of anti-Semitic remarks made by provincial Minister of Agriculture, Mr. Laurent Barré, was perceived as a very positive development by the Canadian Jewish Congress. In its protest against Barré, Canadian Jewish Congress received support from several organizations, but considered as a precedent the condemnation of the politician by the

Archdiocese's representative. With the reply emanating from Mgr. Henri Jeannotte, Chairman of the Comité St. Paul, it was felt that a major step had been taken towards the betterment of relations between Jews and French Catholics.[36]

Monseigneur Charbonneau was often criticized for his influence in the secularization of the University of Montreal. As Chancellor of the University, he tolerated no anti-Semitism or anti-Jewish discrimination. Monseigneur Charbonneau liked to boast of his contribution to making the institution more open towards the Jewish community. Under his authority, he noted that the University provided its first honourary degree to a Jew, in this case the President of Canadian Jewish Congress, Mr. Samuel Bronfman. He recalled the trouble which Jews had in maintaining their status in the Protestant School systems of Outremont and Montreal. He had discussed the matter with the provincial government and had asked them to ensure that Jews were admitted on properly dignified terms.[37]

It should be noted that some regard Monseignor Charbonneau as far less sympathetic to workers and non-Christians than is generally suggested. Historian Conrad Black refers to a letter in which Charbonneau accuses Duplessis of "...a sell-out to the international 'socializing' unions, of taking his cue from a Jewish labour lawyer [emphasis on religious affiliation added by Black] and of imagining abuses against unorganized part-time female piece-work labourers..."[38]

The Evolution of Le Devoir

Amongst the most important accomplishments of Monseigneur Charbonneau, was his influence on the post-war evolution of *Le Devoir*. Under the direction of Georges Pelletier from 1930 through the war period, the newspaper contained numerous anti-Semitic articles. When Pelletier became seriously ill in 1944, *Le Devoir* narrowly escaped falling under the domination of the Union Nationale as several board members of the newspaper were sympathetic to Premier Duplessis. The Archbishop inherited significant shares from Pelletier's successor Jacques Perreault and following Pelletier's death in 1947, Charbonneau acquired additional holdings in the newspaper which enabled him to significantly influence the orientation of the paper.[39]

Charbonneau ultimately turned over control of the newspaper to Gérald Fillion, who hired former Bloc Populaire leader André Laurendeau as a senior colunmist. Both prominent anti-Duplessis nationalists, Fillion and Laurendeau were reevaluating the political and social priorities of French Canada in light of the impact of the war. Rapid demographic and socio-economic changes in Quebec during the war period generated reflection around the basic tenets of French Canadian nationalism. According to one analyst, such slogans as "the cause of the race and the defense of our national culture" elicited less support among the younger generation. Those individuals who twenty years earlier were fervent nationalists were directing greater attention to such issues as state intervention in economic and social matters.[40]

Nonetheless, during the late 1940s, anti-Semitic sentiment was still prevalent amongst a certain element of the French-Canadian elite. In a recent book on the sympathy of some French Canadian politicians and intellectuals for France's pro-fascist regime of Marechal Petain, authorYves Lavertu reveals that anti-Semitic attitudes were pervasive amongst such individuals as Quebec historian Robert Rumilly, former Montreal Mayor Camilien Houde and others. In the case of André Laurendeau, it has been suggested that by 1950 his appreciation and sympathy for the Vichy regime had ended.[41]

Historian Michael Behiels contends that the editors of *Le Devoir* "...found the traditional version [of Quebec nationalism...] defective in several ways and then set out to formulate and disseminate a more progressive, secular and humanist form of nationalism." Gérard Fillion was convinced that no other people in the western world had experienced as rapid or as radical a social change. For his part, in 1952, André Laurendeau wrote:

> At the centre of a universe in revolution, our small world has changed profoundly. We are now fully aware of this situation and are starting to bring new solutions to new problems. These proposed solutions are dividing us. They divide nationalists because their love of the nation and their acute awareness of the dangers facing it do not necessarily imply a set of common options to deal with new questions.[42]

Canadian Jewish Congress officials were encouraged with what they perceived to be a major change at *Le Devoir*. In 1951, the Joint Public Relations Committee was informed of the generally friendlier tone of the French language press towards the Jewish people and their concerns. Noteworthy was an article signed by a journalist at *Le Devoir* who was writing under the pseudonym "Candide." The journalist deeply deplored the anti-Semitism from which Jews in Arab countries were suffering and recognized that unfortunately such prejudices existed in Canada as well and needed to be combatted unrelentingly. CJC officials were aware that Candide was none other than former Bloc Populaire leader André Laurendeau.[43] This was merely one of several occasions following the war in which the editor of *Le Devoir* denounced anti-Semitism. For example, reflecting upon Joseph McCarthy's anti-Semitic diatribes in 1950s America, Laurendeau observed that:

> Après l'assassinat de six millions de Juifs par le régime hitlérien, il ne faut pas avoir l'estomac très délicat pour avaler sans haut-le-coeur ces dénonciations fanatiques. Un tel antisémitisme est si stupide qu'il nous rendrait plutôt philosémites...[44]

He concluded that those responsible for such morbid sentiments against Jews were likely inspired by a sense of self-hatred.

In an article written in *Le Devoir*, Pierre Vigeant described the two main sources of friction between the two groups. They were described as arising from the "keen economic competition the Jews offered to French Canadians and the quite normal difference of opinion on the question of immigration." Vigeant felt that the opposing views did not warrant the charge of anti-Semitism. Finally, he suggested that the Jewish community might accord greater importance to the French language as a consequence of its new interest in the institutions of French Canada.[45]

Reacting to the challenge presented by Vigeant, the front page columnist of the Yiddish daily newspaper, the *Kenader Odler*, endorsed the notion of greater interest among Jews in the French language in order to establish a modus vivendi. It was significant, the *Odler* columnist observed, that "...the suggestion comes from a source, whence we had, in the past, heard altogether different comments in regard to Jews." As for Vigeant's uncompromising stand on the equality of French and English, the columnist was uncertain that with all the good-will in the world they could not satisfy this "autonomist-nationalist" position. Still, Canadian Jewish Congress leadership supported the idea that the Jewish community develop greater interest in the French language and culture.[46]

The Cercle Juif de Langue Française

One of the most significant initiatives in the field of French public relations emerged in the late 1940s, with the creation of the Cercle Juif de Langue Française. Directed primarily by the Canadian Jewish Congress, this body provided the community with a forum for dialogue which extended beyond the clergy and reached the intellectual elite of French Canada during the 1950s. Amongst the founders of the Cercle Juif were David Rome, S.D. Cohen, a founding member of Canadian Jewish Congress, Rabbi Solomon Frank and the director of the *Kenader Odler*, Mr. Israel Rabinovitch.

The Cercle Juif was designed to play an important role in encouraging rapprochement between the Jewish and French Canadian communities. Its very existence was said to be proof that individuals who were neither Catholic nor French Canadian could possess a sincere interest in the French language and culture and work for its promotion. As well, the Cercle Juif would provide an outlet for Jewish Canadians who had significant exposure to Anglo-Saxon culture but maintained an interest in learning more about French culture.[47]

According to the founders of the Cercle Juif, the social structure in the city did not allow sufficient contact between the two groups. In order to facilitate dialogue, the activities of the Cercle Juif would be directed at ameliorating the atmosphere of intercultural relations in Montreal. Opinion leaders were invited to monthly meetings to lead discussions on French culture and to openly assess the relationship between Jewish and French Canadians.

To commemorate the fifth anniversary of the Cercle Juif de Langue

Française in 1952, its Chairman remarked that: "we appreciate that French is in Canada to stay and to flourish. We believe that... the development of the French language and French culture is necessary for national solidarity, for Canadian fraternity."[48] Cohen referred to efforts being made to teach French in the Jewish day schools and French courses being given to Jewish immigrants by the Jewish Immigrant Aid Society of Canada. Finally, reference was made to a statement by Canadian Jewish Congress President, Mr. Samuel Bronfman, to the effect that: "the Canadians of Jewish origin will be the first in our bilingual Canada to defend the rights of the French language as established by the constitution and by Canadian custom."[49]

In that same year, the Canadian Jewish Congress evaluated the work of its French public relations programme and specifically examined both the progress made and continued obstacles which confronted the Jewish community in its relationship with French Canadians. There was a recognition that much of the French community believed that the Jewish residents of the province had a much greater affinity for the English population. They were convinced that such affinity was a deliberate choice and not forced upon them by an exclusionist attitude on the part of the majority. Canadian Jewish Congress officials did not directly address this perception, explaining instead that as a mobile professional and business group whose children largely attended the Protestant School Board, they were more likely to have contacts with the English Protestant group than with the French Catholic community. Public relations work had traditionally been confined to Montreal's, and for that matter Canada's English-speaking residents. Most efforts were, therefore, directed at enlisting the support of English-speaking people of goodwill and to stay close to English language organs of public opinion. All audio-visual material, pamphlets, lectures and press releases were in the English language and most attempts to obtain legislative changes were limited to the Federal government and the provincial administrations of Ontario and Manitoba. This was presumed by many to be the only course to pursue.[50]

In 1952, with the termination of the session of the Cercle Juif for that year, David Rome offered a number of observations on the status of this initiative. In his own terms, Rome contended that "...the baby had grown quite a husky little creature..."[51] Still, Rome felt obliged to alert leadership to potential problems confronting the Cercle Juif. He was concerned with the alarming lack of Jewish attendance at the open meetings of the Cercle Juif and considered this especially problematic given the significant participation of French Canadians in the initiative. By 1952, Rome observed that the imbalance seemed to be corrected and increasingly the same group of Jews and French Canadians attended the meetings.

Above all, Rome was concerned with a very important problem facing the Cercle Juif. As contacts became firmly established between the two groups, he felt that the Montreal Jewish community had to go beyond demonstrating interest in the French language and culture and show a certain measure of achievement in this area. With this goal in mind, it was considered desirable that the Cercle Juif include within its membership, and among those heading it, certain individuals who were familiar with French culture in general and, specifically, French-Canadian culture. Rome concluded that:

> ...we should set about to communicate with reliable persons in our community who are or will be close to the Canadian Jewish Congress, who will be aware of their public relations responsibilities in their participation in the Cercle or who will have the requisite cultural requirements... for the necessary phase of the Cercle programme.[52]

The work of the French Public Relations programme expanded dramatically with the hiring of Naïm Kattan in the year 1954. As a French speaking Jew who had recently arrived from Iraq, Kattan was employed by Canadian Jewish Congress to enhance contacts with the French Canadian population. Few individuals were better placed than Mr. Kattan to pursue such projects. Whereas in previous years, the Cercle Juif de Langue Française had mainly invited clerical leadership to its meetings, Kattan focused on the "forward-looking" intellectual leadership whose ties to the Church had waned and who exerted a growing influence on public opinion primarily through the print media.

Early in 1950, following his public support for the workers involved in a large and widely public labour dispute (the Asbestos Strike), Monseigneur Charbonneau resigned from his position as Archbishop of Montreal. Opposed by many conservative clergyman, Charbonneau's intervention also angered Union Nationale politicians. According to some observers, what became known as the "Charbonneau affair" illustrated the penetration of the Church in secular matters.[53] In the absence of Charbonneau, the Montreal Catholic hierarchy seemed to lack a strong leader to pursue its dialogue with the Quebec Jewish community.

During the mid-1950s, the official dialogue between French Catholic and Jewish leaders came to a rather abrupt halt. In the very midst of "la Semaine de la Fraternité" (Brotherhood Week), the Vatican called upon the co-president of the British Council of Christians and Jews, Cardinal Bernard Griffin, to resign from his position and requested that all Roman Catholics withdraw from the various national branches of the organization. This measure had important repercussions on the Canadian version of the Christian-Jewish dialogue. This directive placed the Canadian Council of Christians and Jews (CCCJ) and its director, Father Stéphane Valiquette, in a precarious situation. After several attempts to seek clarification of the situation from the Catholic hierarchy, Valiquette was instructed to withdraw from his position as director of the CCCJ's Quebec branch. As Valiquette had originally accepted this position on a conditional basis, he prepared the ground for a transfer of responsibility to a secular leader. Wishing to ensure a smooth transition, Valiquette invited the least possible involvement of the Roman Catholic hierarchy in rapprochement efforts between Jews and French Canadians. While the Christian-Jewish Dialogue continued in spite of the British dispute, it saw its credibility severely diminished with the absence of the Catholic hierarchy.[54] This contributed to a shift in the direction of dialogue initiatives pursued by the Quebec Jewish community from the clergy to the journalistic and intellectual communities.

While clerical leaders were by no means excluded from the French-Jewish dialogue, Kattan cultivated relationships with Laurendeau, and with, among others, *Le Devoir* journalist Jean-Marc Léger, the editor of *La Patrie*, Roger Duhamel and CBC journalist René Lévesque, all of whom participated in the work of the Cercle Juif de Langue Française. Perhaps more importantly, with the arrival of Kattan, Canadian Jewish Congress began to publish some of its material in the French language and introduced the Bulletin du Cercle Juif de Langue Française to report on the activities of the Committee.[55]

The leadership of the Montreal Jewish community recognized the importance of sensitizing non-Jewish leadership to the community's major preoccupations. *La Patrie* editorialist, Conrad Langlois, argued that Jewish Canadians were developing a growing interest in French Canada in part inspired by demographic and political considerations. With the regular increase in their numbers and a growing interest in political affairs, French Canadians were becoming a vital force in Canadian politics. With the growth of "Neo-Canadians" and French Canadians and the inevitable decline of the population of British origin, Langlois believed that the two former groups had an interest in making common cause. Langlois predicted that the progress made by French Canadians in the business sector previously dominated by the English population would have a salutary effect on intergroup relationship.[56]

One of the more controversial addresses before the Cercle Juif was given by co-editor of *La Patrie*, Roger Duhamel. President of the SSJB, Duhamel co-operated with Drapeau in campaigns against Jewish immigration in the immediate post-war period. Nearly a decade later, he expressed his bewilderment at how Christians succumbed to the perverse temptation of anti-Semitism. Duhamel added that it was impossible to be a good Christian and an anti-Semite at the same time and those who possessed such sentiments were only disguising their own insecurities. These were important words from someone not immune to such sentiment during his involvement with the Action Nationale, the Bloc Populaire and the SSJB during the thirties and forties.[57]

The Canadian Jewish Congress leadership recognized that the change in attitudes towards the Jewish community did not imply that racial or religious prejudice had disappeared from Quebec. Rather, it was suggested that:

> ...the friends whom we have always had among them have become more active in the presentation of their views. It might

> also be that the Jewish community of Canada has learned with the passage of time and with experience the means of presenting its case more effectively before French Canada and of winning its support.[58]

Like their North American counterparts during the 1950s, many Montreal Jews recognized the necessity of remaining extremely vigilant with respect to anti-Semitic sentiment. Although much progress had been achieved with the French Canadian leadership, much work remained to be done with the broader population. In her 1955 book *Quebec Now*, Miriam Chapin observed a "curious hangover of medieval beliefs among the French Canadians regarding Jews." While observing a great friendliness to Jewish people among most French Canadians, she still noted a lingering presence of anti-Semitism of a political nature with religious overtones.[59]

In the mid-1950s, the Canadian Jewish Congress received a report on relations between French Canadians, English Canadians and Jews. The Centre pour l'Étude des Relations Humaines in Montreal held a series of seminars and conducted an elaborate survey concerning attitudes between the French Canadian, English Canadian and Jewish communities in Montreal. During the course of the study, the researchers discovered that the common sources of anti-Jewish feeling among French Canadians were most often linked to mercantile and business concerns. The view that Jews were not straightforward in their business dealings continued to be widely held by French Canadians in the post-war period. Another stereotype applied to both English Protestants and Jewish Canadians was the perceived tendency to be too materialistic and not sufficiently mindful of cultural or spiritual matters. This, it was felt, would contribute to further secularization of the province. On the economic issues, the author contended that:

> In the larger towns and cities of the province of Quebec, this fear of the Jews on economic grounds has become greatly exaggerated among certain French Canadian groups. It will be remembered that the economic structure of the province is a unique one in which the control over industry and finance

> have largely become concentrated in non-French hands. Since there are a few Jews who have a good deal of power in certain branches of industry and trade, these Jews have become associated in the minds of nationalist French Canadians with the dominant English-Canadian exploiting group. Many French Canadians... have come to imagine that the economic influence... of the Jews in Quebec and in Canada is far greater than it actually is.[60]

Other less formal inquiries into the relationship between French Canadians and Jews were pursued. In November 1957, to celebrate its 50th anniversary, the *Kenader Odler* devoted a special section of its Jubilee edition to relations between French and Jewish Canadians. Several prominent French Canadian and Jewish personalities were asked to respond to two questions formulated by Naïm Kattan.

> (i) The Jewish population of the province of Quebec was manifesting a growing interest in French language and culture. What role might the Jewish community play in the defense of the language and culture and its maintenance and expansion?
>
> (ii) Was it desired and in this case possible to improve relations between French Canadians and English and French Jews? If so, how could this objective be achieved?[61]

Kattan described the context as rife for rapprochement between communities as a result of the economic expansion of the period that had transformed society and better enabled ethnic groups to identify common objectives.

The inquiry also involved a number of French Canadian intellectuals and journalists. The individuals involved represented an important element of French Canadian opinion. They identified three common themes: (1) the need for increased contacts between Jews and French Canadians, (2) the possible benefits to be accrued from defense on the part of the Jews of French language and culture, and (3) the importance of combatting a general sense of indifference that characterized the relationship between the two communities.[62]

For nationalist historian Michel Brunet, the interest of Jewish leadership in French language and culture could not have been manifested at a more appropriate time. One of the more influential historians of the period, Brunet was the author of "Trois dominantes de la pensée canadienne-française" which described traditional Quebec society as influenced primarily by agriculturalism, messianism and anti-statism. He noted that the French Canadian people would have to take some major steps to promote their collective life that corresponded to technological and social advances taking place. The interest of the Jewish population could serve in what he regarded as the struggle of the French Canadian population since the British conquest to preserve a distinct society in the valley of the St. Lawrence.

Brunet regarded the continuing enrolment of Jews in both the Law Faculty and Dentistry Department at the University of Montreal as desirable and a potentially important vehicle for rapprochement efforts as they contributed to multiply the possibilities for contact between French Canadian and Jewish professionals. It was the elites which, according to Brunet, had the principal responsibility for encouraging these rapprochement initiatives. He concluded that francophone Jews would ultimately take the lead in familiarising their Anglo-Jewish counterparts with French Canadian society. The support of the Jewish community would help alter the perception that only French Canadians were interested in the permanence of the French fact in North America. Feeling less isolated, the French Canadians would become more confident and show greater appreciation for inter-ethnic relations.[63]

For *La Patrie* editorialist Conrad Langlois, in order for "Neo-Canadians" to feel completely at home in Quebec, it would be vital for them to learn the French language. This was true for the Montreal Jewish community in order to improve relations with French Canadians. According to Langlois:

> Les Juifs devraient, par exemple, cesser de donner, presque partout, une façade anglaise, des airs de Canadiens anglais unilingues. Il n'y a rien qui pourrait nuire davantage à leurs

intérêts dans la province du Québec que l'adoption par les Juifs de l'anglais comme langue unique.

Langlois believed it was essential to multiply the degree of interaction between Jews and French Canadians and that the continued use of the French language was the best way to achieve this objective. It was critical to terminate the continued process of anglicization of Jewish immigrants. While Langlois recognized that ongoing contact existed between bilingual French Canadians and unilingual anglophone Jews, he added that these encounters could benefit from greater knowledge of the French language which would improve access for many Jews to a larger segment of the French Canadian population. Langlois maintained that "on ne peut comprendre vraiment la mentalité des Canadiens-français et les valeurs canadiennes-françaises... qu'en se familiarisant avec la langue parlée de la population de la province du Québec."[64]

For his part, Father Richard Ares, Director of the Jesuit review *Relations* viewed with great enthusiasm the idea of Jews defending the French language and culture in Canada, a responsibility which had fallen exclusively on the French Canadians for approximately 200 years. Ares believed that the use of the French language by more members of the Jewish community would help facilitate the process of *rapprochement*. While the acquisition of the language often required a certain amount of goodwill, he believed that the Jewish community did not lack this quality. Ares felt that the Jewish community should be guarded in its economic interaction with French Canadians so as to avert any exploitation. It was in this sector of activity where Ares believed that stereotypes had been formed.[65]

One of the most interesting opinions on the subject of rapprochement was submitted by the director of the Canadian Council of Christians and Jews, Mr. Roger Lapointe. He believed that any effort among Jews to promote French would remain moribund without improvement in the relationship between Jews and French Canadians. He felt that improvement was not only desirable and possible but also not without a sense of urgency. Little was to be accomplished, he believed, unless each group made a commitment to reduce mutually held prejudices. Until the Jews and French Canadians made more effort to demystify one another's cultures and did so inspired by humane rather than academic interest, progress would be slow. The common character of Canadian citizenship was stressed by Lapointe. Multiplying individual contacts was essential. He maintained that:

> Si l'on admet que les préjudices les plus dévastateurs se repassent de généralisations portant sur des groupes, on devra convenir également que rien n'est aussi efficace pour les détruire que de bonnes relations individuelles d'un groupe à l'autre.[66]

Canadian Jewish Congress Executive Director, Saul Hayes, suggested that the Jews of Canada would be one of the first groups to be interested in the language, culture and traditions of French Canada. He believed that the two communities were natural allies and maintained that the national aspirations of French Canadians, highlighted by their desire to maintain their language and culture, resonated in the spirit of Jews whose personality was also characterized by the slogan "Je me souviens" and possessing their proper version of "our language, our institutions and our laws." Hayes went so far as to conclude that:

> ...groups should undcrstand that by working towards the integrity of the cultural sovereignty of French Canada, they would be rendering themselves a service...[67]

Conclusion

On the front page of the January, 1955 edition of the newsletter of the Cercle Juif, Montreal Mayor Jean Drapeau was photographed alongside Canadian Jewish Congress President Samuel Bronfman and the Chief Rabbi of Israel, Isaac Halevi Herzog. Under most circumstances, Drapeau's presence among these Jewish dignitaries would not have been surprising. Still, it may have been paradoxical for those who knew Drapeau at another time in his career when he spearheaded actions that were detrimental if not hostile to the Jewish community.[68]

In a speech delivered at Westmount's Temple Emanu-el in February of 1955, Mayor Drapeau praised the contribution of ethnic groups to the growth and importance of the Metropolis. These remarks were widely reported and attracted the attention of the Montreal Jewish community. In the company of Toronto's Jewish Mayor, Nathan Phillips, Mayor Drapeau emphasized the level of mutual comprehension which characterized the relationship between the city's ethnic communities. He reserved particular praise for the initiatives of the Cercle Juif de Langue Française of Canadian Jewish Congress, whose programme of dialogue between Jews and French Canadians contributed significantly to combatting prejudice and reducing tension between the leadership of the two groups.[69]

Drapeau represents but one example of a change in attitude towards Jews exhibited by certain French Canadians as they found themselves in positions of authority during the post-war period. In their public relations initiatives, Jewish community leaders fully recognized the need to work with individuals and institutions that were once perceived to be problematic. In the aftermath of the Holocaust, the opportunities for sensitizing non-Jewish leadership to Jewish community concerns expanded greatly throughout North America. French Canada was no exception.

Seeking to change its image, Quebec's Roman Catholic clergy entered into a sort of partnership with certain Montreal Jewish leaders aimed at the improvement of relations and the elimination of "...the vice of anti-Semitism and the false attitudes which prejudice breeds..."[70] Prior to the war, the Roman Catholic Church was to a significant extent responsible for the spread of anti-Jewish feeling. Thus in the late 1940s, the message of tolerance most certainly confused some of its followers. Indeed, the liberalism displayed by Monseigneur Charbonneau ultimately constituted a threat to the prevailing political authorities. Consequently, as certain leading French Canadian clerics experienced a decline in their influence over the population and a more secular expression of Quebec nationalism emerged, the Jewish community modified its public relations strategy. While not excluding ties with Quebec clergy, outreach to French Canadians by the mid-1950s, was primarily directed at intellectuals, editorialists and literary and cultural figures.

During the 1960s, *Le Devoir* editor Claude Ryan argued that it was essential for Jews to have a better idea of French Canadian life and for young French Canadians to learn about Jews beyond what was transmitted by the media (a treatment which Ryan noted, had vastly improved since the war). Ryan deemed it essential for Jews to become more involved in the debate within the French Canadian community about the future of Quebec society. He concluded that:

> I know a lot of Jews who keep asking questions about where French Canadian nationalism is going... If more people of different backgrounds were involved in these very fundamental interrogations that are being raised at this moment in the French Canadian community, it would help to pose the questions in a more moderate tone, in a more complete way that would be a better reflection of all aspects and facets of reality.[71]

Through the Cercle Juif de Langue Française, the Jewish community's elites offered the possibility of confronting the aforementioned challenge. Yet, such initiatives always appeared fragile because of their relatively limited degree of support from the Jewish community and the ability of only a select group of individuals to successfully lead them. With the Quiet Revolution and the emergence of Vatican II, Montreal's Jewish leadership felt there was a lesser sense of urgency around rapprochement efforts. With the 1960 electoral victory of the provincial Liberals and the defeat of the Union Nationale, the Jewish community felt the climate was such that avenues for the presentation of community concerns and exchange of views had shifted somewhat to the political front. With the departure of Naïm Kattan in the early sixties, the Cercle Juif de Langue Française quickly ceased to exist. Its absence clearly constituted a setback towards efforts for Jews and French Canadians to reinforce existing partnerships.

Notes

1. Yossi Levy, "Profil d'un pionnier de l'intercultural: Jacques Langlais, C.J.C." dans *Horizons Interculturels*, Hiver/Printemps 1993, no: 29, 35.

2. Michael Brown, *Jew or Juif? Jews, French Canadians and Anglo-Canadians, 1759-1914*, Philadelphia: The Jewish Publication Society, 1986; David Rome and Jacques Langlais, *Jews and French Quebecers: Two Hundred Years of Shared History*, Sir Wilfrid Laurier University Press, 1991 and Pierre Anctil, *Le Rendez-Vous Manqué: Les Juifs de Montréal Face au Québec de l'Entre Deux Guerres*, Montréal: Institut Québécois de recherche sur la Culture, 1988.

3. Irving Howe, *World of our Fathers: The Journey of the East European Jews to America and the Life They Found and Made*, New York: Simon and Schuster Publishers, 1976, 630.

4. Rome and Langlais, *op. cit.*, 112 and 114.

5. Gerald Tulchinsky, "The Third Solitude: A.M. Klein's Jewish Montreal, 1910-1950" in *Journal of Canadian Studies*, volume 19, no. 2, Summer 1984, 96-112 and Peter Desbarats: see Chapter "The World Between" in *The State of Quebec: A Journalist's View of the Quiet Revolution*, Toronto: McClelland and Stewart, 1965.

6. "The Attitude of the French Canadians Towards the English Canadians and Towards the Jews," unpublished essay submitted to the Bulletin of the Canadian Jewish Congress. CJC National Executive Director, Saul Hayes, described the author as a newspaper man who for years has lived in the milieu of French intellectual and political life, CJC National Archives 2B Collection, S.D. Cohen.

7. Harold E. Quinley and Charles Y. Glock, *Anti-Semitism in America*, New York: MacMillan Publishing, 1979. The authors report who in a 1945 survey, 1 in 4 Americans would vote for a candidate that was "against the Jews."

8. Esther Deslisle, *Le Traître et le Juif: Lionel Groulx, Le Devoir et le délire du nationalisme dans la province de Québec, 1929-1939*, Montréal: L'Étincelle Éditeur, 1992.

9. Paul-André Linteau et al., *Quebec Since 1930*, Toronto: James Lorimer and Company Publishers, 1991, 80. For anti-Semitism of *Le Devoir*, see Deslisle, op. cit.

10. Linteau et al..., op. cit., 80.

11. Anctil, "Le Rendez-Vous manqué...," op. cit., 263.

12. Ibid, 236-240.

13. Ibid.

14. Tulchinsky, "The Third Solitude...," op. cit., 105 and Jack Jedwab, "Uniting Uptowners and Downtowners: The Jewish Electorate and Quebec Provincial Politics, 1927-1939" in Canadian Ethnic Studies, XVIII, 2, 1986.

15. Bernard Figler, Q.C., *Biography of Louis Fitch, 1889-1956*, Montreal, 1968, 46-50.

16. Canadian Jewish Chronicle, October 14, 1938, 3.

17. Figler, "Fitch ...", op. cit., 51.

18. André Laurendeau, *Witness for Quebec*, Toronto: Macmillan of Canada, 1973, 32-33. See also the editorial of A.M. Klein in the Canadian Jewish Chronicle, April 24, 1942.

19. Moses W. Steinberg and Usher Caplan, eds. A.M. Klein, *Beyond Sambation: Selected Essays and Editorials*, 1928-1955, Toronto: University of Toronto Press, 1982, 141.

20. Ibid.

21. Laurendeau, "Witness...," op. cit., 71-72.

22. Ibid.

23. Ibid, 72.

24. Michael Oliver, *The Passionate Debate: The Social and Political Ideas of Quebec Nationalism, 1920-1945*, Montreal: Véhicule Press, 1991, 180.

25. Irving Abella and Harold Troper, *None is too Many: Canada and the Jews of Europe, 1933-1948*, Toronto: Lester and Orpen Dennys Publishers, 1983, 231. His biographer, Conrad Black, added that: Whether he believed it or merely exploited the limitless fears and latent anti-Semitism of rural Catholic Quebec, the whole despicable episode was probably the shabbiest in his political life of more than 40 years... This was the only act of anti-Semitism Duplessis ever committed and there is no evidence that he harboured such sentiments on a consistent basis.

26. Robert Rumilly, *Histoire de la Société Saint-Jean-Baptiste de Montréal*, Montréal: Editions de l'Aurore, 1975. 530.

27 *Canadian Jewish Chronicle*, December 29, 1944 and also Steinberg and Caplan, *op. cit.*, 230.

28. Conrad Black, *Duplessis*, Toronto: McClelland and Stewart, 1977, Chapter 10.

29. Ibid, 502.

30. Ibid.

31. Report for Dominion Council Meeting, Eastern Division on *Work of Committee on French Canadian Groups*, "Memorandum", Canadian Jewish

Congress, Montreal, December 4, 1947, Canadian Jewish Congress National Archives, 2B Collection, S.D. Cohen. The memo indicates that the Public Relations work of the CJC had been initiated by David Rome.

32. "Memo": *Roman Catholic Church in Canada*, which examines attitudes towards Jewish community, c. 1952, CJC National Archives 2B Collection; S.D. Cohen.

33. Ibid.

34. Ibid.

35. "Memo": *The Public Relations Committee program among Roman Catholics and French Canadians*, c. 1952, CJC National Archives 2B Collection, S.D. Cohen.

36. "Memo": *The Hon. Laurent Barré*, c. 1952, CJC National Archives 2B Collection, S.D. Cohen.

37. "Memo": *The Public Relations Committee...*, *op. cit.*

38. Black *op. cit.* 527.

39. Michael D. Behiels, *Prelude to Quebec's Quiet Revolution: Liberation versus Neo-Nationalism, 1945-1960*, Kingston: McGill-Queen's University Press, 1985, 22.

40. Ibid, 36.

41. Yves Laverty *L'Affaire Bernonville: Le Québec face à Petain et à la Collaboration* (1948-1951) 16 éditeur, Montréal: 1994 Lavertu looks at the campaign waged by several Quebec opinion leaders to prevent the expulsion from Canada of French war criminal, Jacques de Bernonville. For Laurendeau's change of heart, see the preface to the book written by André Malavoy.

42. Ibid, 37-38.

43. *Memorandum* to the Dominion Council, Eastern Region of the Canadian Jewish Congress, Montreal, May 22, 1951.

44. André Laurendeau, "Bloc-Notes" in *Le Devoir*, 28 novembre 1952.

45. Ibid.

46. Ibid.

47. "Édition du Jubilée d'Or—Golden Jubilee Edition," *Jewish Daily Eagle*, (Montreal), November 22, 1957, 41.

48. "Statement of S.D. Cohen, one of the founders of the Cercle Juif de la Langue Française," c. 1952, 1, CJC National Archives 2B Collection; S.D. Cohen. This statement was prominently published in *Le Canada* and in *Le Devoir* as well as other newspapers.

49. Ibid.

50. "Remarks on Public Relations for open meeting," December 2, 1954, CJC National Archives 2B Collection; S.D. Cohen.

51. *Memorandum* from David Rome to Saul Hayes and S.D. Cohen, "Re: Cercle Juif de Langue Française," Montreal, Canadian Jewish Congress, June 9, 1952.

52. Ibid.

53. Cameron Nish, *Quebec in the Duplessis Era, 1935-1959: Dictatorship or Democracy?*, Toronto: Copp Clark Publishing Company, 1970, 106.

54. Stéphane Valiquette, S.J., *Mémoires Judéo-Chrétiens d'Un Jésuite Canadien, 1912-1990*, Bibliothèque Nationale du Québec, Montréal, Canada, 1990, 37.

55. For René Lévesque, see *Bulletin du Cercle Juif de Langue Française*, No. 52, février 1960, 11; for Jean-Marie Léger, see *Bulletin du Cercle Juif de Langue Française*, No. 4, février 1955, 2; and for Roger Duhamel, see *Bulletin du Cercle Juif de Langue Française*, No. 2, décembre 1954, 2.

56. "Édition du Jubilée d'Or—Golden Jubilee Edition," *Jewish Daily Eagle*, November 22, 1957, 38.

57. "A la dernière réunion du Cercle Juif, M. Roger Duhamel attaque l'antisémitisme" in *Bulletin du Cercle Juif de Langue Française*, décembre 1954, No. 2, 2.

58. Pierre Anctil, "A.M. Klein: du poète et de ses rapports avec le Québec français" in *Journal of Canadian Studies*, volume 19, no. 2, Summer 1984, 122.

59. Miriam Chapin, *Quebec Now*, Toronto: The Ryerson Press, 1955, 161-162.

60. "The Attitude of the French Canadians Towards the English Canadians and Towards the Jews," Canadian Jewish Congress National Archives 2B Collection, S.D. Cohen, May 1954.

61. "Éditions du Jubilée d'or—Golden Jubilee Edition," see "Enquête sur: Les Relations entre les Canadiens Français et les Juif," Jewish Daily Eagle, *op. cit.*, 36.

62. Ibid.

63. "Michel Brunet," Ibid, 38.

64. "Conrad Langlois," Ibid, 38-39.

65. "Richard Ares," Ibid, 37.

66. "Roger Lapointe," Ibid, 39.

67. "Saul Hayes," Ibid, 36.

68. Michael D. Behiels, *Prelude to Quebec's Quiet Revolution: Liberation*

versus Neo-Nationalism, 1945-1960, Kingston: McGill-Queen's University Press, 1985, 22.

69. *Bulletin du Cercle Juif*, No. 3, Janvier 1955, 2.

70. "Memo": *Roman Catholic Church...*, *op. cit.*

71. Claude Ryan, "A French Canadian Looks at the Jews," *Viewpoints*, Vol. IV, No. 3, October 1969, 13.

Safeguarding a Distinctive Identity
Hasidic Jews in Montreal

WILLIAM SHAFFIR

TO MODERN OBSERVERS of Jewish life, the Hasidim pose a profound enigma: their communities survive, even flourish, in the midst of assimilating tendencies characterizing the larger Jewish community.[1] Despite overwhelming odds that their lifestyle could not be sustained in an urban secular environment, Hasidim cling tenaciously to a way of life, steeped in *halachic* principle, distinctive customs and traditional practices, and deeply committed to traditionalism. The story is told that when the first cohort of Lubavitcher Hasidim arrived in Montreal in 1941, the wagering among Jews was whether their children would successfully withstand the secularizing influences of the host culture. They did and accomplished this feat very successfully. They have managed to carefully shape the socialization of their young, and the community boasts a series of educational, religious, and economic institutions which ranks it exceptionally high along the lines of institutional completeness.[2] Defections are rare, the divorce and separation rates remain remarkably low, and traditional male-female relations remain intact. Carefully channelling its members' social interaction and social life, and instituting effective measures of social control, the Hasidim have cultivated and maintained a highly distinctive identity.

This essay examines two dimensions of identity maintenance among the Hasidim by which they preserve their distinctive way of life. Borrowing from Barth,[3] I employ the concept of boundary-maintaining mechanisms to investigate two concrete features of this process—the organization of secular education, and the role of proselytization as it pertains to the Lubavitcher Hasidim.[4] The two components or properties of boundary work to which I address myself do not apply equally to each of the sects. The organization of institutions to channel and control members' activities is a feature common to all of the Hasidic sects, but the form both of the institutions as well as the channelling will differ between the sects. Proselytizing, or the coordination of out-reach activity within the larger Jewish community, is the hallmark of the Lubavitcher Hasidim and is organized at the local level as well as at the world headquarters of Lubavitch in Crown Heights, Brooklyn. This is not to suggest, however, that followers of other Hasidic sects absolutely refrain from such activity. However, when such activity occurs among Hasidic sects other than Lubavitch it is not organized at the community level but is, instead, initiated and conducted by individuals.

Background

While seemingly the same to uninitiated outsiders, the Hasidim do not constitute a uniform group but are divided into a number of distinctive sects. While commonly committed to the observance of Orthodox Jewish law, the sects may differ in details of attitudes, customs and beliefs as well as commitment to the teaching of their particular *rebbe* or charismatic religious leader.[5] It is, therefore, only in a loose sense that the Hasidim constitute one community.

Although a few Hasidim resided in Montreal prior to the Second World War, their substantial influx to the city effectively began in the late 1940s and early 1950s. Both because of its proximity to New York—the centre of Hasidic life in North America—as well as an established infrastructure of Hasidic institutions and economic opportunities in Quebec, the Hasidic population of Montreal has increased over the past decade, numbering today approximately 4,000 persons. The city includes followers of ten sects—Bobov, Belz, Klausenburg, Lubavitch, Munkatch, Papa, Satmar, Square, Tash, and Vishnitz. The three most recently arrived sects—Munkatch, Papa, and Square—number approximately 30, 20, and 50 families respectively. The Bobover and Klausenburger Hasidim have remained relatively small, numbering approximately 20 and 15 families respectively, while the Vishnitzer, numbering some twenty families in the early 1970s, have tripled in size.

The largest Hasidic sects in Montreal are Lubavitch, Satmar, Belz, and Tash. The Satmar and Belzer Hasidim have memberships of some 150 families, the Tasher include about 120 families, and the Lubavitch sect, the largest, numbers about 225 families. Despite their growing numbers, the Hasidic residential concentration within the city has not altered substantially since their arrival. With the exception of the Tasher sect which relocated to the municipality of Boisbriand outside of the city to establish a colony, the majority reside in an area which is bounded by Fairmount St. to the south, Van Horne to the north, St. Urbain to the east, and Jeanne Mance to the west—the boundaries which marked the Jewish community until the mid-1950s. Although the Lubavitch sect initially settled in this same area, its followers relocated to the Snowdon district of the city in the early 1960s shortly after the Jewish community commenced its relocation to more westerly and suburban areas.

Boundaries and the Preservation of a Distinctive Identity

Despite the presence of ideological and social differences characterizing the various Hasidic groups in the city, all attach great importance to preventing assimilation by insulating their members from the secular influences of the host culture—a theme commonly addressed in ethnographic studies of Hasidic sects.[6] An essential question, then, relates to how the various sects are organized to ensure that their respective boundaries remain secure. As Kanter has observed, boundaries not only define a group, setting it off from its environment but, in giving it a sharp focus, also facilitate commitment.[7] In an early reference to boundary maintenance, Loomis and Beagle link the activity to identity retention. Boundary maintenance, they assert, "... is the process whereby the system retains its identity and interaction pattern; that is, retains its equilibrium involving both integration and solidity."[8] Along this line, Frederik Barth's formulation of boundaries is especially useful.[9]

Despres has observed that "... one is tempted to consider ethnic studies B.B. or A.B. (i.e. Before or After Barth)."[10] To him, as well as to numerous social scientists, it was Barth's formulation of the concept of 'ethnic group boundary' that provided the starting point for a more theoretically interesting work on ethnicity.[11] "If a group maintains its identity when its members interact with others," writes Barth, "this entails criteria for determining membership and ways of signalling membership and exclusion".[12] Entailed in boundary maintenance are situations of social contact between persons of different cultures, in this case between Hasidim and outsiders, both Jewish and Gentile. However, as long as all members of the group consider themselves to be members and frequently interact with other group members on a primary level, while keeping the rest of the society at arm's length, the ethnic boundary is maintained.

Barth's concept of ethnic boundaries was innovative because it suggested that it may actually be ethnic boundaries, rather than the structures enclosed within these boundaries, which both primarily define ethnic groups and account for much of the dynamics of ethnic persistence.[13] According to Barth, a group boundary represents a criterion of membership which marks off a continuing unit,[14] and his discussion of ethnic boundaries identifies two interacting sets of influences which affect group boundaries—one which facilitates the integration of a group, and another which differentiates a group from other groups. According to Barth, ethnic boundaries persist despite the flow of personnel across them partly because ethnic boundaries may be based on identities and ascribed characteristics which are often independent of contemporary or transient social situations, and because ethnic identities and ascriptions are not characteristics which individuals can readily discard. An application of Barth's formulation suggests that the viability of the Hasidic community as an identifiable entity is shaped by the presence of marked differences of behavior—cultural and social structural differences—distinguishing them from outsiders. Thus, the persistence of boundaries requires not only criteria and signals for identification, but also a structuring of interaction allowing for the perpetuation of cultural differences. As such the strategy most commonly used by the Hasidim both to cultivate and maintain a distinctive identity is by insulating themselves from outsiders.

The exotic customs of the Hasidim are used in part as a protective fence around their community. By distinguishing themselves from the gentiles and nonreligious Jews, the Hasidim believe that they can best preserve their identity, keep their children from becoming acculturated, and prevent possible infractions of the religious law. This need to maintain their insularity is a recurrent theme in Hasidic tradition.[15]

The Coordination of the Secular Curriculum[16]

> One day, in a discussion with the chief rabbi, I told him: Three hundred years and you haven't changed. You still wear the same clothes and everything. It boggles my mind...." He told me: "Listen, if you have a nice piece of furniture that has been there three hundred years, you're not just going to sand it and make it into any old piece that you can buy in the store...." See, you get his idea here. These are things we cherish, not suffer through. You have to be proud of your parents and grandparents, and what they left you. You have to nourish it and keep it alive. So I understand this philosophy, build on it and try to teach these kids as much as possible without breaking down any of their values [secular principal of a Hasidic school].
>
> A Tasher pamphlet printed in English reads: "The Tasher community is living proof that one need not have advanced degrees in secular studies in order to succeed. Although the yeshiva and girls' school do teach French, English, and mathematics and other secular subjects, the Rebbe does not place too much emphasis on these."

Like other Hasidic sects, the Tasher maintain that secular education threatens their traditional values; and in order to shield their children against its potentially harmful influences, they run their own schools where secular classes are closely supervised to ensure that the pupils will not see any conflict with the contents of their religious studies. In fact, several of the Hasidic sects in Montreal, including Lubavitch,

Satmar, Belz, Tash, and Square have established their own schools and, in each case, in accordance with the principle of separating the sexes, separate schools are maintained for boys and girls. Of these schools, those of Lubavitch, Square and Belz receive subsidies from the Quebec provincial government which requires that they provide a minimal number of hours of instruction in French per week and that the secular studies curriculum is accredited by the Provincial Ministry of Education. The Satmar and Tash schools have long refused any school subsidies from the government because they do not wish to comply with the obligations entailed. As a Satmar school official explained: "Were it [the school] subsidized, then there'd be a minimum of three hours per day of secular studies.... They don't want to be obliged to be exposed to things they don't want their children exposed to." In this respect, the objective of this program, but particularly for the boys who, following the completion of the Grade 6 level terminate their secular studies, is oriented around practicality. A school principal explained: "All they want is to know how to read, how to write, mathematics, a bit of geography, a bit of French to communicate.... They want the basic language to communicate, to get along in society.... And they need it for business because most of them become businessmen."

That secular education is viewed as a potentially negative influence can affect the choice of outsiders who are hired to teach. These schools must look to the outside to staff their secular departments as their own graduates lack the necessary qualifications to provide such instruction. While school officials claim to be primary interested in applicants' educational qualifications, less formal criteria may serve as important considerations in the hiring decision. When the ideal secular teacher—a practising Orthodox Jew with a teacher's certificate—is difficult to find, Gentiles may be hired in preference to nonreligious Jews, believing the former to be less likely to sway students, intentionally or otherwise, from their religious beliefs. As matters currently stand, almost all of the staff in the boys' secular studies programs are Jewish,and are either Orthodox or traditional in their religious identification.

To help ensure that students' religious beliefs are not challenged by the secular materials, teachers are specifically instructed about the constraints within which they must conduct their work. Typically, they receive verbal instructions from the principal concerning the topics that are proscribed. As one administrator remarked:

> Teachers are told that we don't expect them to talk about boys and girls. Girls have their activities and boys have activities, but not together. You wouldn't talk about sex or anything that has to do with reproduction. Or boyfriends, girlfriends, birthdays. Then there's the great theories—evolution and the creation of the world millions of years ago. We don't get into these conflicts. A secular teacher does not talk about religion. It's out of his field. That's the way we lessen the friction.

As well, however, to make matters even more formal, proscriptive discussion topics and methods of instruction may be distributed to the staff in written form. What follows are the written directives to the secular staff in the Tasher and Satmarer schools:

[Tasher]

1. All textbooks and literature to be used by the students in class or at home for extra-curricular activities, etc. must first be approved by the principal.
2. No stencil or photocopy of any other book may be used without the principal's approval.
3. Students are not permitted to go to the library nor is the teacher permitted to bring into the school, for the students, such books.
4. No newspaper or magazine may be read in school or hung up. Students are not permitted to read the above at home either.
5. No record or tape may be used in the classroom without the approval of the principal.
6. No extra subjects, books, magazine supplement or other information which is not on the required curriculum of the school may be taught.

7. For extra credit work or for class projects, etc., students should not be told to write away for such material. The teacher should supply them with the material with the principal's approval.
8. No discussions on boyfriends.
9. No discussions on reproduction.
10. No discussions about radio, TV or movies.
11. No discussions about personal life.
12. No discussions on religion.
13. No discussions on women's lib.

[Satmarer]

1. Every book, workbook, reading book, which is used in the classroom by the teacher or the students has to be checked and approved by the religious committee appointed by the school; the teacher is not allowed to bring or advise the students to use any book which is not given by the school.
2. No stencil or photocopy of any book except school books which are stamped approved are allowed.
3. Sending students to libraries or reading to students from library books is strictly forbidden.
4. No reading of Newspapers is allowed in class. The teacher should not encourage the students to read newspapers; only publications approved by the school are permitted in the classroom.
5. No tapes or record [sic] are allowed in the classroom.
6. All books are strictly edited from harmful influences according to our religion. If you notice anything which might have been overlooked, please notify us promptly.
7. No subjects, books, magazines supplements, information which have not been given to you by the school are to be taught or brought to school.
8. When setting up school projects, all ordering of materials is to be done by our office staff.
9. Avoid discussing any subject involving Zionism or the State of Israel.

> 10. Do not speak Hebrew.
> 11. Do not talk about boyfriend-girlfriend-parties and so on.
> 12. Do not discuss adult subjects which are not for children.
> 13. Do not discuss radio, television, movies, theatres, which you might have heard or seen on these with the students.
> 14. Do not discuss your private life with the students.
> 15. Do not discuss any religious subject, including the Jewish faith.
> 16. No homework should be given before a Jewish holiday.
> 17. Any discussion or story regarding boy-girl relationship, romance, sexual problems; sexual organs; etc... is strictly forbidden.
> 18. Please behave in school in a way befitting for a religious school such as dressing and talking in a modest way.
> 19. Certain subjects should never be discussed when in the classroom: the theory of evolution; the creation of the world...

These instructions demonstrate the stringent measures taken to ensure that children are neither acquainted with nor, worse still, exposed to ways deviating from a strict Hasidic lifestyle. They are complemented by a censorship applied both to the selection of books for classroom use as well as the specific material that such books may include.

The attention invested in the selection of appropriate textbooks naturally involves a detailed screening of the material. To paraphrase one of the school administrators, stories told to the children must not include 'ultra-modern' views. As an example of what he considered harmful, he offered the example of a tale about a Jewish boy who was a pupil in a non-Jewish school. The boy was eventually accepted for the baseball team; and on one Saturday they came to pick him up to play on that day but his father refused to let him go. The administrator commented:

> Now that's a game that we think a boy shouldn't have on his mind, that he could go and play baseball on Shabbess [the Sabbath] afternoon.... I'm not saying that that's the worst

example of a story that might be passed [over]. But there are stories that have sex in them, and things like that which are totally out.

The particular techniques for screening the material range from substituting certain words, phrases or sentences in a story with more appropriate ones, to the actual removal of the pages. A principal offers an example of the former:

> A teacher finds a story and I read it. I say: "Okay, remove this word." We try not to lose the idea, the context, but we change certain words. [Can you think of an example of a word that you'd change?] Television. "At night he went to the living room and watched television," you'd change that to: "At night he went to the living room and read a book." So we take white ink, cover it and write on top of it.

A more extreme form of the screening process, short of deleting the pages, involves inking out, with black marker, any written or pictorial content that are deemed to be offensive. A principal comments:

> Sometimes they've [the rabbis] gone over parts of it [a story] in black with a marker.... Usually it happens in the geography book when they talk about fossils that are a million years old because it would come into contradiction with everything they're learning.... [Do you also censor pictures in books?] ... you can't see a woman with her arms bare, you can't see a woman wearing pants. So usually you try to find drawings rather than real life pictures. But in a subject such as geography you have pictures of people, streets.... So usually with a marker you go over things you don't want them to see.

The particular techniques used for screening varies according to the predilections of the individual(s) charged with that responsibility. For instance, one such individual censored photographs which showed women and even young girls dressed immodestly by inking them out in black pen. By contrast, another Hasidic administrator considered it unnecessary to ink out pictures of little girls who were not wearing socks, especially when it was clear from the context that the girl was a Gentile. As he explained:

> Our kids are aware that the goyim [Gentiles] do not dress the way we dress.... I mean, if you're reading a story about goyim, then you know that goyim don't wear socks. As long as it's not a mini skirt or anything like that, it's o.k. It's no use blacking everything out.

Yet another technique—the one typically adopted by the Lubavitcher—is to refrain from excising but to simply substitute something suitable for the objectionable material.

With the exception of the Lubavitch school, the secular educational experience is limited to the classroom. Only occasionally are students expected to complete assignments at home, the time for which should not exceed fifteen minutes. Extra-curricular activities, which offer too many temptations to secular involvement are simply discouraged. As one principal explained:

> No, we don't even talk about public libraries. We don't encourage students to go to public libraries because then they'd be exposed to all kinds of literature that's not censored. We don't even mention libraries, we don't mention newspapers.... You have to be careful about what you bring in. Newspapers are out, publications are out. No audio-visual equipment. We work like in a jungle—a few books here and there. We have a blackboard.

In the end, however, the Hasidim are aware of the impossibility of shielding their students from all potentially disruptive secular influences. Teachers and parents alike view such influences as the inevitable accompaniments of secular education and both hope and expect that the school's religious studies programme will offset them.[17] As an intentionally organized mechanism of social control, the coordination of secular studies helps the Hasidim to maintain the boundaries separating them from the surrounding culture.

The Proselytizing of Lubavitch

To any observer of the Hasidic scene, Lubavitcher are set apart, and set themselves apart from the other Hasidic sects by their outreach practices with other Jews, regardless of the latter's degree of Jewish observance. In an attempt to fortify the boundaries surrounding their communities, the Hasidim, as a rule, do not encourage and, indeed, even discourage outsiders from mingling in their institutions. As such, the case of the Lubavitcher Hasidim, who actively and extensively proselytize in the larger Jewish community, is apparently very puzzling.

A self-proclaimed historical landmark of this sect, the proselytizing work of the Lubavitcher Hasidim has increased dramatically over the past few decades. During the period of the late 1960s, Lubavitch was mainly identified with a Tefillin Campaign.[18] The Tefillin campaign was initiated by the Lubavitcher *rebbe* and, while endorsed by much of the larger orthodox community, became associated with Lubavitch. It started shortly before the outbreak of the Six Day War in the Middle East in 1967 when the *rebbe* urged his followers throughout the world to ensure that as many Jews as possible observed this precept. Its observance, claimed the *rebbe*, would inevitably aid the Jews in Israel, especially those in the army, in their war with the enemy. Pamphlets and newspaper advertisements in the English and Yiddish press extended invitations to people to perform this commandment at the Lubavitch yeshiva or at other synagogues. The Lubavitcher carefully coordinated a witnessing drive to reach as many Jews as possible. In addition to approaching Jews at cultural gatherings, Tefillin booths were established at Jewish locations, such as shopping malls and plazas known to attract a mainly Jewish clientele. Trucks, decorated with slogans urging Jews to don *tefillin*, were aptly called by Lubavitcher 'Tefillin mobiles' or 'Tefillin tanks.' To be expected, the community's growth in size has resulted in a proliferation of outreach-type activities and the creation of new institutions to facilitate such work. In short, the Lubavitcher have become increasingly skilled at helping Jews to identify with, and to become committed to, an Orthodox Jewish lifestyle. To mention but some of the institutions organized by Lubavitch in the city, there are: seven Chabad houses or drop-in centres for Jewish youth and adults located in various parts of Montreal [Chabad is an acronym for *Chochmoh* (wisdom), *Beenoh* (understanding), and *Daas* (knowledge)—the three basic principles elucidated by the first Lubavitcher *rebbe* in his interpretation of Judaism as a way to God; Chabad and Lubavitch are synonymous, referring to the same Hasidic sect]; eight telephone numbers for 'Torah-on-the-Line' where the caller receives a message about a particular Torah portion; educational classes for various age groups—men and women—relating to specific facets of Orthodox Judaism; an Encounter with Chabad weekend program geared for college and university students; an Institute For Brides and Grooms to inform soon-to-be marrieds about the Jewish laws regulating marriage and the family; two summer camps and two day schools—one for boys, the other for girls; a public celebration of the Channukah (Festival of Lights) festival, including a motorcade parade and the lighting of huge Hanukkah candelabra strategically located throughout the city.

While the actual practice of proselytizing is not officially delegated to any specific age group, many of the organized activities involve the participation of the older yeshiva students—the *bocherim*—ranging in age from fifteen to nineteen. Thus, for example, while all Lubavitcher were interested in the Tefillin Campaign's success, these older students were mainly responsible for visiting college campuses to contact Jewish youth. The organization of such activity, including numerous others in which they were involved, called for their interaction with outsiders which could easily expose them to situations inimical to Orthodox Judaism. Unlike this age-group among the Satmarer Hasidim, for example, whose leaders have institutionalized their separation from unobservant Jews and indeed all outsiders, Lubavitcher *bocherim* regularly devote periods of time to making the acquaintances of, and even befriending Jews whose observance of Jewish law is minimal.

It is commonly believed that witnessing, especially among those who challenge a group member's set of beliefs, is a threat to the group's identity. Confronted by sceptics, the disinterested, and non-believers, the individual may come to question and eventually doubt the set of principles around which he has organized his identity. It is for this very reason that certain groups and communities trying to cultivate and maintain a distinctive identity have intentionally segregated themselves from the larger society by minimizing their members' contact with outside influences.

While one effect of witnessing is its immediate threat to the group member, a less obvious result is that, in fact, it strengthens the very self-concept that it is believed to weaken. Far from threatening the group's efforts to maintain and consolidate its identity by blurring and eroding the boundaries, witnessing serves to reinforce the distinctive identity both at the individual and community levels. As Mol has observed: "Every act of witnessing anchors the belief system deeply in the motions of the believer, since faith has to be proclaimed against the non-believer. The boundaries around the belief system are thus firmly drawn."[19]

On the surface, then, it might appear that Lubavitchers' proselytizing, and their acceptance of outsiders into the community's institutions, such as their schools and summer camps, potentially dilutes the clarity of these Hasidim's self-definition by threatening the preservation of a distinctive identity through diluting the communal boundaries. It can be argued, however, that Lubavitchers' contacts with nonreligious Jews serve, in fact, to reinforce the sect's distinctive identity. While an analysis of the manifest consequences of proselytizing may show the activity to be largely ineffective—for instance, few newcomers are actually added to the group, and the number of Jews appreciably influenced by the Lubavitcher is small—it is its latent consequences which contribute to the group's persistence.

Festinger et al., in their study of a religious cult, the Seekers, suggest that if the group's central beliefs are either questioned or not believed by others, proselytizing is an effective means of reaffirming the member's identity with the group. As the writers state: "If more and more people can be persuaded that the system of belief is correct, then it clearly must, after all, be correct."[20] While Lubavitcher might concede that an overwhelming proportion of Jews neither practice Orthodox Judaism nor share their convictions concerning their *rebbe*, whom they regard as the central figure in Jewish life today, they would, nonetheless, claim that they are making extraordinarily swift progress in these directions. Plentiful stories abound of prominent and ordinary men and women who have, for the first time, donned phylacteries or lit Sabbath candles, and have koshered their home in accordance with Jewish dietary laws. For Lubavitcher, these activities symbolize an important beginning to what, hopefully, will result in an ever-increasing identification with, and commitment to, Orthodox Judaism. Both the in-roads and successes created by their proselytizing are always current topics of conversation and are featured in local and national Lubavitch publications. Through their network of communication, Lubavitcher are familiar with the names of politicians and entertainment personalities who seek to meet, and be photographed with, their *rebbe*, and who publicly endorse the spiritual contribution made by these Hasidim to the quality of Jewish life on the world scene. Coca Cola and Lubavitch, claim these Hasidim, are two commodities that can be found everywhere in the world—a testimony both to the success and zeal of their proselytizing work.

An important philosophical foundation of the Lubavitch movement, and one that has served as a motivating force for its missionary zeal, is its teaching that no Jew is ever lost to God. Within every Jew, so the teaching goes, there is a point of authentic Jewish faith, *dos pintelle Yeed*. As Weiner, writing about the Lubavitcher, and recounting a conversation with one of its chief administrative officials, observed: "One has to remember that the soul itself was so much deeper than what appeared to the eye," and hence surface appearances ought never to discourage one from attempting to tap a man's inner capacity for faith in and love for Judaism."[21] When he inquired of this official the number of Lubavitch followers in the world, the rabbi replied: "How many Jews are there in the world?"

The Thomas theorem, "If men define situations as real, they are real in their consequences,"[22] can be modified to state that if a community collectively defines a situation to be real, its members will organize their behavior accordingly. Defining all Jews as readily susceptible to the tenets of Orthodox Judaism, and encouraged by continuous streams of reports of Jews' intensified determination to adopt *halakhic* principles, Lubavitcher Hasidim become increasingly committed to participating in the multitude of witnessing activities coordinated by their community. At this point, any objective evidence indicating that relatively few Jews are seriously, or even slightly, affected by the Lubavitch outreach work hardly impacts upon these Hasidim's definition of the situation. More specifically, while the definition of the situation may be false, several mechanisms are set into motion leading to behavior that makes the prediction come through; in short, their behavior is characterized by a self-fulfilling prophecy.

We can now understand better how witnessing consolidates the Lubavitcher Hasidim's identity. It is precisely the act of witnessing in the larger Jewish community that reinforces the members' beliefs and enables the community to retain its specific boundaries. When a Lubavitcher attempts to influence and convince a non-observant Jew of Orthodox Judaism's relevance, he is, in fact, influencing and convincing himself. This is so because, as Mead observed, a person can act socially toward himself just as he acts toward others and can thus become the object of his own actions.[23] By discussing and arguing with others about their *rebbe*'s accomplishments, or the lasting significance of Torah observance, Lubavitcher must think about the facts and arguments themselves, thereby reinforcing their identity. It is in this manner that proselytizing activity can be related to matters of identity and boundary maintenance.

Conclusion

Despite a perception of the Hasidic community as relatively static and as largely unresponsive to major societal changes over the past decade, a more precise appraisal of this society is that, much like the Hutterites, it is "... an ongoing socio-cultural entity constantly adapting to environmental, political, and social circumstances and at the same time realizing the opportunities which their particular configuration offers."[24] The Hasidic community is best investigated in terms of the dynamic interplay between the various sects' institutional organization and the continuous evaluation of the perceived threat of foreign influences; in short, what may be conceptualized as boundary-maintaining activity. Such activity requires an assessment of one's current practices and their continued suitability, and can be initiated either at the individual level or by collectivities within the community charged with the responsibility of preserving a distinctive identity.

In this essay, I have only begun to detail some of the dynamics relating to boundary-maintaining devices among the Hasidim and have mainly focused on such devices as they pertain to outsiders. Further research employing the boundary metaphor could investigate whether certain Hasidic communities rely more heavily on certain boundary-maintaining devices than on others, as well as on inter-Hasidic boundary-maintenance devices enabling the respective sects to preserve a measure of distinctiveness. Such analyses should help to capture the processes by which the Montreal Hasidic community is increasing in numbers, experiences few defections, and is skilfully transmitting its values and traditions to successive generations.

Notes

The research for this paper has been supported by a grant from the Social Sciences and Humanities Research Council of Canada. A more extensive version of this paper is scheduled to be published in Janet Belcove-Shalin, *Hasidic Ethnography Today*. New York: SUNY Press.

1. Steven M. Cohen, *American Modernity and Jewish Identities*. London: Tavistock, 1983. *American Assimilation or Jewish Revival?* Bloomington: Indiana University Press, 1988. C. Goldscheider, *Jewish Continuity and Change*. Bloomington: Indiana University Press, 1986. C. Goldscheider, and A. Zuckermann, *The Transformation of the Jews*. Chicago: University of Chicago Press, 1984.

2. R. Breton, "Institutional completeness of ethnic communities and the personal relations of immigrants." *American Journal of Sociology*, 1964:70, 193-205.

3. F. Barth, *Ethnic Groups and Boundaries*. Boston: Little, Brown and Company, 1969.

4. One can cite additional institutions within the Hasidic community which feature prominently in boundary work including, for instance, the family, the *bays-medresh*, or study hall, the yeshiva, and the *mikveh* (ritual bath). Most significantly, however, is the role of the *rebbe* who serves as a sect's

charismatic leader as he directs its affairs and who in his relationship to his followers "... functions in the uncertain areas of life rather than in the clearly defined domain of the law" J. Mintz, *Legends of the Hasidim*. Chicago: University of Chicago Press. 1968, 89. In this regard, the *rebbe* serves as a central agent of social control whose outlook and philosophy shape the contours of a particular Hasidic sect's social, economic, and political boundaries. For an interesting analysis of the Lubavitcher rebbe's role and the institutionalization of his charismatic leadership, Sydelle Brooks Levy, "Ethnic Boundedness and the Institutionalization of Charisma: A Study Of The Lubavitcher Hassidim." Unpublished doctoral dissertation. University Microfilm, Ann Arbor, Michigan, 1973.

5. J. Gutwirth, "Fieldwork method and the sociology of Jews: case studies of Hasidic communities." *The Jewish Journal of Sociology* 20 (1) 1978, 49-58.

6. J. Gutwirth, *Vie Juive Traditionnelle: Ethnologie d'Une Communaute Hassidique*. Paris: Les Editions De Minuit, 1970. J. Mintz, *Legends of the Hasidim*. Chicago: University of Chicago Press, 1968. S. Poll, *The Hasidic Community of Williamsburg*. New York: The Free Press, 1962. I. Rubin, *Satmar: An Island in the City*. Chicago: Quadrangle Books, 1974. W. Shaffir, *Life In A Religious Community: The Lubavitcher Chassidim in Montreal*. Toronto: Holt, Rinehart and Winston of Canada, 1974.

7. R. Kanter, *Commitment and Community: Communes and Utopias in Sociological Perspective*. Cambridge, Mass.: Harvard University Press, 1972.

8. C. Loomis and J. Beagle, *Rural Sociology: The Strategy of Change*. Englewood Cliffs, N.J.: Prentice-Hall, 1957.

9. F. Barth, *Ethnic Groups and Boundaries*. Boston: Little, Brown and Company, 1969.

10. L. Despres, "Towards a theory of ethnic phenomena." L. Despres (ed.) *Ethnicity and Resource Competition in a Plural Society*, 187-207 The Hague: Mouton Publishers, 1975.

11. Along a related line, the process encompassed by Barth's formulation has been addressed by Breton. In focusing on the character of social and institutional boundaries between groups, he refers to a phenomenon of enclosure by which is meant "...the existence of social boundaries between groups and to the mechanisms for the maintenance of these boundaries..." and "... a particular pattern in the contours of such boundaries". R. Breton, "Stratification and conflict between ethnolinguistic communities with different social structures." *Canadian Review of Sociology and Anthropology* 15 (2) 1978, 148-157.

12. F. Barth, *Ethnic Groups and Boundaries*. Boston: Little, Brown and Company, 1969.

13. Ibid.

14. Ibid.

15. J. Mintz, *Legends of the Hasidim*. Chicago: University of Chicago Press, 1968.

16. The coordination of secular studies differs for males and females, and my discussion focuses on the former. As a general rule, the secular program for females is more extensive than for males, not only lasting longer both in terms of hours of instruction per day and grade level completed but also in terms of the range of subjects that are covered. As in the case for the boys, however, the contents are screened and the secular teachers are closely supervised.

17. In recent years there has been greater support for the secular program from the religious authorities. This is best attributable to the realization of the complexity of economic life and the necessity to be familiar with changing expectations. As one of the secular principals explains: "Look, they realize that it's not like before where if you opened a business then you could hire one bookkeeper. You better know how to manage your business instead of relying totally on someone else. But also in terms of simple matters: the street signs are all in French and you won't know where to park your car if you can't read them." The extent of the change must be kept in proper perspective. Characterizing this change, another principal cautioned against exaggerating its magnitude: "There was a kind of evolution in the last few years, but nothing revolutionary. Just a slight movement, barely noticeable."

18. The observance of *tefillin* is incumbent on all Jewish males who have reached the age of thirteen. The *tefillin*, or phylacteries, consist of two small leather cubes, each containing a piece of parchment inscribed with specific Biblical verses. They are worn by men during the morning religious services on days other than the Sabbath and holy days, one strapped to the left arm, the other to the forehead. To popularize the observance of *tefillin*, Lubavitcher organized a *tefillin* campaign which became their single-most successful proselytizing activity in the late 1960s.

19. H. Mol, *Identity and the Sacred: A Sketch for a New Social-Scientific Theory of Religion*. Agincourt: The Book Society of Canada Ltd, 1976.

20. L. Festinger, H.W. Riecken and S. Schachter, *When Prophecy Fails*. New York: Harper and Row, 1956.

21. H. Weiner, *9 1/2 Mystics: The Kabbala Today*. New York: Holt, Rinehart and Winston, 1969.
22. W.I. Thomas and D.S. Thomas, *The Child in America*. New York: Alfred A. Knopf, 1928.
23. G.H. Mead, *Mind, Self and Society*. Chicago: University of Chicago Press, 1934.
24. K. Peter, *The Dynamics of Hutterite Society*. Edmonton: The University of Alberta Press, 1987.

Moroccan Jews and Their Adaptation to Montreal Life

JOSEPH LEVY
YOLANDE COHEN

ONE OF THE MAJOR CHARACTERISTICS of modern Jewry stems from the important demographic changes accompanying the end of World War II, the creation of the state of Israel and the independence of Arab countries in the Machrek and Maghreb. The rise of nationalism in these regions and the tensions of the Middle-East have contributed to feelings of insecurity on the part of the Jews of these regions and increased their movements of migration, practically emptying these countries of their Jewish population. In search of new havens and socio-economic progress, this population settled in new host countries: France, Spain, Israel, the United States and Canada, particularly in Toronto and Montreal. Moroccan Jews began to settle in Montreal around 1965, but it was after the Six-Day War, that their number, today around 15,000, increased rapidly. Because of its ethno-cultural characteristics, this group was confronted with a particular situation. On one hand it shared with the Québécois majority a common language, French. On the other hand, through its Jewish origins, it had some historico-religious affinities with the local English-speaking group of Ashkenazi Jews, whose communal perspectives were nevertheless in conflict with its own.[1] Several studies done on this group have helped to understand their institutional structure,[2] the religious components of their identity, their relationship to Israel[3] and their economic and socio-psychological adaptation.[4] However, quantitative methodologies, while important, do not always enable us to understand more the subjective dimensions linked to their adaptation to their new socio-cultural environment. The use of more qualitative approaches, based mainly on life-history and testimonies can help to ascertain the affective and ideological components which underline the emigration process and its impact on family structures, socio-economic networks as well as the ecological and social perceptions of the host country. We chose to use this ethno-historical approach in our research on the Moroccan Jews in Montreal whose preliminary results were presented in a book based on a limited number of biographies.[5] We will here focus on the process of Moroccan Jews' adaptation to Montreal by using oral data provided by the analysis of thirty interviews obtained from informants of both sexes and different generations.[6] This methodology, which has been used in other studies on Jews of France, Algeria and Turkey provides a plethora of data,[7] in spite of some of its limits: gaps in the life stories, selection of facts, distortion and reinterpretation of the past, idealisation, and insistence on the collective aspects of migration, instead of more personal dimensions. Nevertheless, in spite of these constraints, these interviews help to present more vividly the intense experiences linked to the uprooting and the cultural shocks which accompany the integration to a new country. Our objective here will be to examine the perceptions of immigration and adaptation to Montreal life, as seen through the eyes of some of the migrants. Following the analysis related to their general perceptions of their new country we will examine the characteristics of their three main strategies of adaptation which can be defined as nostalgia, mimetism and ambivalence.

Perception of Canada

The emigration of the Moroccan Jews marked the end of a Jewish presence of more than a thousand years in the Moroccan landscape. It portended deep changes in the emigrants' identity, according to each country of immigration. A first question is obvious: why choose Canada instead of Israel, with its religious attractions, or France, whose culture and language had attracted many Moroccan Jews? Among the myths of Israel as the promised land and France as a country of culture, Canada is associated with the myth of America: a land of freedom and money, mixed with folkloric elements gathered from movies, books and songs. The political problems specific to Québécois society—such as the rise of the nationalist movement or the linguistic quarrels between Anglophones and Francophones—are rarely mentioned in the interviews and do not appear to have been considered as a dimension underlying the decision to emigrate. Canada is essentially perceived as a land of immigration, of economic opportunities, of freedom and abundance, while Quebec, is perceived as a French-speaking province, open to immigration, far from the tumult of nationalism and conflict. These themes pervade the majority of the biographies; our informants have the strong feeling they were welcomed and that they could easily belong to their new country:

> Canada is a country of immigration. It belongs to no one, it belongs to the immigrants which inhabit it. We are all immigrants, we have built this country. (male, senior citizen)

> I like Canada. Here is everything we want. (female, senior citizen)

> In Canada, naturally it is freedom which is important. It is to be able to say that I could do what I wanted, to find work immediately, even if I earn three times less than what I earned in Morocco. When we talk of Canada, we talk of a new country where everything is possible. We talk of the immensity of this country while the large metropolises are still average cities when compared to large European or American cities. What attracts people here is maybe the myth of America. I think that the only attractive thing in this country is a feeling of freedom. (male, forties)

> I have the feeling that Canada belongs to no one. For me, it's a host country for all and no one can claim it. (male, thirties)

> Life here is easier. There is all the comfort possible. We are living very well. We do not lack anything. We cannot say we

> cannot buy something. Thanks to God, we are very well and we live comfortably. (female, senior citizen)

> Canada is a free country where one can develop as he pleases. (male, twenties)

The emigrants' ignorance of the Canadian past, which easily translated into the North American myth of the self-made man (which lacks any historical or political perspective), is pervasive. It allows them to conceive that they arrived in a virgin land, that is, to consider that they did not have to go through a socialization process. And if they would have to do so, at least it would not be as complete as the French one for example, or for that matter even the more disruptive Israeli one (military service being a radical form of socialization). So it seems to them that their identification with a country that has so little identity to impose will be easy.

They even suggest that being part of this country has brought then individual pride since it eliminated the feelings of insecurity that surrounded their life in Morocco. The freedom to follow their religion is seen as an essential freedom; it permitted the affirmation of Judaism, without fear or inhibition.

> There was no more insecurity as in Morocco, none at all. Here, we can hold our heads high. (female, senior citizen)

> We should give thanks to this country for having welcomed us and given us our dignity back to be a man and a Jew. (male, senior citizen)

> Canada is an extraordinary country. It is a country which enables you to be Jewish. We eat kosher with no problems. We can do Shabbat... Here in Montreal, I assume my identity, I have no shyness, no shame. (male, thirties)

The question of the climate and its seasonal modulations, winter and cold are dominant in the interviews, but they are perceived differently, depending on who speaks and what they do:

> In winter, I suffer. I am very chilly. I often stay at home. I dress warmly. (male, senior citizen)

> We have everything we want... in quantity of snow. I am not cold. The houses are heated. It is much better than in Morocco. (female, senior citizen)

> The cold, the snow, the temperature do not affect me, I adapted immediately to the climate. (female, senior citizen)

> What I regret most from Morocco, like many, is the climate; I need more sunshine and the winter here is too long. (male, forties)

> I had neither a climatic nor a cultural shock when I came here. I loved the snow and jumped into it as if I had always been used to it. I started skiing. (female, fifties)

> In the beginning, we expected winter to be very hard. In fact, it was quite easy for everyone. (female, thirties)

Nostalgia

As noted by Elbaz: "The relationship to the country of origin is symbolized by a present-absent space. Place of birth, of a time where the transmission of Judaism derived from codes dictated by the past, constitutes the primary reference....Nostalgia is a recurrent theme in the interviews. It appears magnified, probably because the uprooting did not occur in the midst of agony or tragedy, as was the case for the European Jews, or in humiliation, as it was for their Israeli counterparts."[8]

The theme of nostalgia essentially dominates the life-stories of the older persons and constitutes an important leitmotif, as is shown in the following two extracts:

> When they talk of Morocco, my parents always say wonderful things. They make you want to go and see this country. It's always superb, it's always a good life and, once in a while, when they get impatient, they say: Ah, if only we stayed in Morocco! (male, twenties)

> Yes, there is nostalgia. Because you know, in Morocco, we lived a full life. I have to say that we were ignorant, because we did not know, we did not appreciate the life that God and the country had given to us. We had to leave Morocco to notice the difference between the life of the past and the life of the present. (male, forties)

For the older people — whose reasons for immigration were essentially related to family networks, to join a brother, a sister or children —the memory of a strong and structured community, and an identity rooted in a Judeo-Arabic tradition which modulated all dimensions of everyday life, serve as elements of comparison between the society of origin and the host country. They contrast the richness of their social and familial ties in Morocco to the isolation and solitude they often experience in Montreal, and which they break by immersing themselves in their neighborhood, in their community institutions and synagogues or by developing new networks. It is also hard for them to develop new friends or a different pattern of sociability; their old habits do not really fit with the new ones:

> I don't have many friends... I go to cafés, to the mall, I sit on a bench, I meet people, I often talk about Torah... Unfortunately, I do not have any family. Even my only brother does not invite me for Shabbat because he knows I do not take the bus on that day. (male, senior citizen)

> In Morocco, I was used to having thousands of friends who came to my home. I went to their house, there were always people around our home—Muslims, Jews, Christians—but here, it's not the same, so we learned to get along without it.

Not happily, though. In the beginning, it was very depressing. (male, senior citizen)

I had many friends in Morocco, but I did not have a single friend here. So my children registered me for the golden age club of the Sephardi community. Then, I went out with my daughter and her friends, and I adapted myself. (female, senior citizen)

The emigrants' relationships to other ethno-cultural groups, apart from the Jews, and to the Québécois population are limited and their history is ignored:

Among the Québécois, there is good and bad, as everywhere. Most of them are not real Québécois. We give them the name of Québécois, even though they are not, they live in Québec. They might be Hindus, Haitians, they can be from all origins. As to the francophone Québécois, we do not have much contact with them. (male, senior citizen)

The question of linguistic adaptation, although rare, is also the object of criticism and wonderment:

What shocks me in this country, is that wherever I go, I cannot talk because I am not bilingual. I do not speak English. The majority of people, instead of speaking French, speak English. I thought Québec was French, so I was very happy to communicate with people, but it's not the case and I find myself handicapped. (female, senior citizen)

The norms of behavior in the Canadian society, and, especially, the sexual freedom enjoyed by women in Québec are also an important concern for some informants:

I pray for my son to find a virtuous wife for him alone, with no mixing. Yes, yes, I know what I am saying, today there are a

> lot of mixing, tonight she sleeps with him and tomorrow with another. Like a bowl of honey, whoever comes by dips his fingers and tastes. God forbid! (female, senior citizen)

The cycle of the holidays continues to constitute an important facet of the respondents' existence. Their maintenance of traditions aims to maintain a semblance of continuity with the past, notwithstanding the transformations linked to the environment and to the reorganisation of the family network. However the comparison with the atmosphere of the holidays in Morocco often diminishes the pleasure and brings back old memories of a lost golden age:

> I still observe all our traditions for the holidays, specially the meals. (female, senior citizen)

> When he talks of Passover in Morocco, my father always says: "the air smelled of Passover." There was something in the air and for Mimouna, he reminds us of how special it was there. To listen to him compare, you would think it was always better there than here. (male, thirties)

Mimetism

The second mechanism of adaptation can be defined as mimetism, that is, a desire to integrate to their new country, to understand its specificity, its problems and to adopt the patterns of leisure and consumption specific to the American way of life. For the generation between thirty-five and fifty-five years old, the reasons for immigrating are not linked to external constraints but to internal motivations: a strong will to distance themselves from the myths of the Judeo-Arabic golden age and the idea of paradise dominant among the older respondents. Emigration is not considered as exile. It rather is a response to a lucid analysis of the political situation of Morocco, as well as the international situation. The limits of social and economical status, that is the chances of upward mobility, are also taken into consideration in the decision to emigrate. In Morocco, as in all integrated societies, hierarchies predominate and restrain mobility.

The state of the relations between Jews and Muslims is also evaluated. While on the surface, they still seem friendly, the tensions originating from the Middle-East conflict affect the general atmosphere, leading to a deep insecurity and accelerating departure:

> Of course they were Muslims, and there was the Israeli-Arab conflict... This conflict was finished. Because freedom no longer existed for us Jews. As Jews, we had something less than the Muslims. We were not entirely Moroccan. And I could not accept it. That's what made me decide to leave Morocco. (male, forties)

> After the Six Day war, there was a wind of panic and my sister asked my parents to seriously consider Canada, because the situation was too worrisome... We first attempted to leave Morocco for professional reasons. My husband had finished his studies and, at that period, it was difficult to find work. It was taking too much time and it was worrying us, because we could not see any future. Of course it was not official, but we had already assumed that the Jews of Morocco would not stay. (female, fifties)

> My parents were not at ease in Morocco... I think it was because of the Arabs. Our parents could see there was no future and they were more afraid for us, the children, than anything. My father would have stayed there for financial reasons: but he had four children and no future. (female, thirties)

Immigration was therefore considered to be a serious matter. Many who came to Canada had previously been living in France, for relatively long periods of time, before crossing the Atlantic. Many decided to immigrate after a touristic visit, a visit to parents or even spontaneously:

> Parisian friends of mine emigrated to Montreal and invited us to visit them. They had mentioned the Expo of Montreal,

which encouraged us to come. We were not really impressed by Canada... We had come as tourists... Later, we obtained our visas for the United States. I told my husband why don't we pass by Montreal? If it doesn't click, we can always go to the United States. It was a period where people started talking about Canada. We felt that things were happening there... And the fact that French was spoken gave the country a different colour. (female, fifties)

We were then in the thick of the hippie movement and travelling a lot was part of its philosophy. One day. I walked by the Canadian embassy in France with a friend. We said let's ask for our immigration papers and we would try to visit America. We asked for a form that we sent by mail and forgot about it. A few months later, the embassy informed me that my request had been granted. I arrived in Canada, without knowing anyone. (male, thirties)

By exploring the possibilities offered by a society where they thought immigration was the rule, the newcomers discovered the multiple facets of freedom. Originating mostly, although not exclusively, from Moroccan upper-middle classes, they spoke French well enough and many came with secondary or university degrees. They often possessed a cultural and professional background that they used to create new business or professional opportunities. Their goals were not achieved without difficulties, due to the absence of Canadian job experience which, sometimes, slowed down their entry into the job market or necessitated several professional reorientations:

I was hired as a designer on the Olympic stadium project, which was a short-lived project. From this moment, I constantly changed jobs. I went from salesman to manager in a cosmetic products company. (male, forties)

My husband took courses offered to immigrants for a few months. They were an initiation to Canadian life and he was given English courses... the director asked him if he did not want to teach English to immigrants... he learned the method and started teaching... He registered for a Masters in linguistics and became a teacher...

I found work immediately. I did some secretarial work and I found a good position in a newspaper. I worked in the editing room and then with the general director... I went to the University of Montreal and obtained a diploma in translation. (female, fifties)

While they wholeheartedly accept the North-American liberal code that permits the expression of professional qualities, this perspective still arouses conflicting points of views as to its costs, even if achievement remains a dominant goal.

> In terms of work, I think the North American system lacks sentiment. It is a very demanding country at the work place. So you must be strong in everything. You must be professional everywhere. You cannot afford to be mediocre... I was given the opportunity to prove myself, and that was the nice side of Canada. (male, forties)

> The people were more open, more serene. Life was more calm than in Marseilles. I understood very quickly that they trusted the individual more than in Morocco or France. (male, forties)

> In Montreal, life is so difficult that people tend to change for the worse. They become more selfish, tougher. They become nasty. (man, forties)

Learning about freedom through mimetism, the individuals of this generation do not hesitate to adopt local values. Rapport with society becomes closer while contacts with Montrealers are more frequent and more appreciated, going as far as mixed marriages:

> The people were very understanding. I have not had a bad experience in twenty years. I was often told of racist events in the workforce. Personally I have never felt it. People knew I was Jewish. It was funny, I found myself very close to the Québécois. Their mentality was relatively close to ours, to us Moroccans: warm, appreciating the good things in life. (female, fifties)

> Canadians are very hospitable, particularly the French-Canadians. When I went to look for work, I was never told no. In my workplace, it is half francophone, half anglophone. It is especially agreeable to work with a francophone clientele. They are less mistrustful, they talk more easily, they are less inhibited. On the other hand, on the anglophone side, I find they have more culture and more weight....But in terms of personality, I prefer to mingle with francophones, it's warmer, more agreeable. (male, forties)

This relationship to the host society does not interfere deeply with the relationships they continue to have with the Moroccan Jewish community whose institutions, developed in the 1970s, permitted the maintenance of an ethno-cultural specificity which ensured a warm sociability, a conviviality that they wanted to perpetuate and renew:

> I have French-Canadian friends, English-Canadian friends but I also feel the need to live in my community... We surely will lose the interpersonal links we had in Morocco, this warmth which will exist no longer, unless we preserve it. That's what we are trying to do by creating schools like Maimonides... Some might accuse us of living in a ghetto, but I don't think it is the case. I am open to the larger society, but I have this need to find myself with my Moroccan friends, in Moroccan activities. I need my children to learn what I learned in Morocco. (male, forties)

> Since our close friends and immediate family are not in

Montreal, we have befriended new people in the Moroccan Jewish community. We do things together. There was a great enthusiasm because, maybe mistakenly, we thought we were pioneers. (female, fifties)

Judaism takes on different forms: for some, it is defined by a respect for the major traditions, or, often, in terms of Jewishness without religious connotations:

I feel strongly Jewish, but I do not practice at all. That's all. We do not miss the holidays. On the other hand, if friends invite us, we are very happy. For Passover, I go to my parents' home, because it is important for them. (female, fifties)

For others, on the contrary, Québec, enabled them to fulfill religious aspirations which are expressed by maintaining a strict religious life or in certain cases, by returning to an orthodox way of life, which ensures Jewish survival:

I have been very active for a long time in Jewish milieus and I am presently working in one of the institutions of the community not so much to keep my Jewish identity which, I believe, is well rooted in me, but to transmit a message to my children. And I want this message not to be biased like the one our parents have given us since they acted differently than what they were preaching. (male, forties)

The respondents' relationship to Israel is an important one, since this country, where they often have friends and family, constitutes an essential component in the definition of their identity. This concurs with the conclusions of Elbaz (1989) as to the centrality of Israel in the construction of the Jewish identity of the Moroccans living in Montreal:

Even having immigrated to Canada, I felt as a Jew, that something in me was missing where Israel is concerned. That is why as soon as I had the opportunity, I travelled to Israel. My Jewish feeling and my belonging to Judaism and to the state of Israel are very strong. (male, forties)

I remember working for the Combined Jewish Appeal. There was no francophone section at the time. We continued to participate in certain demonstrations in the community, but we were not active in the organisation, except when there were problems, in the case of Israel for example. For years, I somewhat idealized this country... I never went there. I never wanted to go to Israel to visit family, go to the Wailing Wall and to the beach. For me, Israel means other things. (female, fifties)

For this generation, therefore, the ideal is one of synthesis between traditional values and modernity. Personal success is embedded in a community context and integration into the Montreal community does not jeopardize Moroccan Jewish identity. That identity is reorganized by taking into account the constraints of the new environment. For many, Montreal remains a place where they can anchor themselves, without abandoning their roots. Notwithstanding this successful adaptation, the future is not always perceived in an optimistic light, since the sovereigntist claims in Quebec are perceived through the mirror of their experience of Moroccan nationalism and their fear of renewed anti-Semitism:

In the long-term, I will have to leave once again. I don't think the situation will stay like this. You need to be objective. If they do not have independence now, it will be in ten years. There will be problems, like we had problems in Morocco... I am convinced that we will have to leave for the United States or the Canadian West. If I was a Catholic francophone, there would be no problems, but, tomorrow, there will certainly be anti-Semitism if Quebec makes its own laws. (male, forties)

Ambivalence

For the generation that was born and grew up in Quebec or immigrated at an early age or at adolescence, the problems of adaptation are expressed differently. The basis of their Moroccan identity is not linked to a nostalgic past or to a deep experience of Moroccan life, as with their elders. Their insertion into Montreal, on the surface successful, raises many questions.

For many, one of the first shocks they experienced was related to their entrance into the Protestant schools, where English as a language of education clashed with French, the family language, and for many the maternal language. Furthermore lack of knowledge about Moroccan culture is prevalent:

> In the beginning when I was going to Protestant school, I was totally lost. I didn't know anything. When the teacher would say "what is your name", I would answer "Hélène." She would not understand. I had to apply myself to pronounce it the English way. It took me some time to learn to pronounce it, to answer to the teacher when she would call out a name that was not mine. (female, thirties)

> When I came here, I went to the Protestant School Board in a French school. In the classes, the students would ask me: are there camels, dromedaries that walk around in your country? They thought that but I never understood why. They thought I came from an underdeveloped country. (male, twenties)

For others, the French accent provoked teasing towards them:

> For me, arriving in Canada was like arriving in France: I felt humiliated in school. They asked me a question and I answered with my very Parisian accent, and then the class burst out laughing: "Ah, the bloody French!" It was insane. I had an accent that was not mine and on top of that I would get insulted. I didn't know where I stood then. Was I French? Was I Moroccan? Did I need to become Moroccan again? I come to France,

> and they treat me as a Moroccan. I come to Quebec, and they calll me "Bloody French!" (male, twenties)

Attendance at Maimonides school, one of the francophone Sephardic schools, seems to bring less tensions, a situation which is probably related to its homogeneous social fabric, at one and the same time protective but also often too narrow:

> Today with the distance of time, I conclude that Maimonides was, in general, a good school. It was almost like a family... Even though it was a good school, it was still a private school, relatively closed. I wanted to go to a public school and maybe open myself up a bit. (male, twenties)

> I went to Sephardic school in St-Laurent for two months. My mother did not like it at all. Then I was accepted at Maimonides where I spent the best years of my life with my friends. (male, twenties)

The CEGEP milieu is also experienced in contradictory ways since its pedagogical orientation requires more autonomy and responsibility, values which could clash with the more traditional perspective prevalent in Maimonides school, thus creating difficulties for some students:

> CEGEP was a very bad period. In Maimonides, in Secondary 4 or 5, we started to skip school; we wanted more freedom. In CEGEP we had this freedom. We took advantage of it and we dropped our courses. This freedom was too much, especially when you come from a traditional private school where you knew the same people during the primary school. (male, twenties)

> In CEGEP, I very much liked this freedom of taking yourself in hand, to be fully responsible of one's self. That's what I was looking for and what I was missing at Maimonides. I found it

extremely different than Maimonides which was a pretty closed milieu. (male, twenties)

> Here, you have to do everything by yourself and depend only on yourself. I feel more capable, more responsible; it demands a lot more energy; it gives worries before time, but it doesn't matter, it's stimulating. (male, twenties)

As for their elders, achievement remains a dominant value. Most often, they enter the job market at a young age to earn some pocket money, working on the weekend in shoe or clothing stores, some of them deciding to drop out of school, temporarily or permanently, in order to work and ultimately to go into business. University studies in fields that lead to professional jobs and an interesting career are still important for many. Material success then becomes synonymous with acquiring a recognized profession which assures a rapid social progression in a changing society where competition is severe but challenging:

> At this moment, I am working on a Masters in Marketing. I would like to work in an enterprise in marketing or publicity, because I like it very much. I am very optimistic about my chances of finding a job. (male, twenties)

> I find that the young Moroccans of my generation get along very well in Canada and it is very encouraging. Many Moroccans have good diplomas and I am sure they will succeed in life. It's a brilliant success considering that our parents did not get a chance to study extensively. (male, twenties)

Some contrasts are evident between those who feel they were not integrated to the Montreal society, continuing to maintain a relative closure towards the host society, and those who open themselves to the surrounding society and attempt to understand it:

> When I came to Canada, it was different. Let's say I felt a

stranger, and to this day I feel a stranger. (male, twenties)

In Morocco, I felt insecure, I felt Jewish, whereas here I feel human, as everyone else. I never heard "Dirty Jew", but it's for certain that jokes on Jews are made. It's so painful. (male, twenties)

My contacts with the francophone Québécois? To tell you the truth I do not have any. (male, twenties)

It was my first contact with the Québécois. I hadn't known anyone until I went to CEGEP, but even there contact was restricted. I never managed to approach them. I don't say I don't like them, it's that I find no common interests with them. Presently, I hang around with some Québécois, but there is always a barrier. I am sure of that. It's because I am not a Québécois. Maybe the accent plays a role... I live well in my milieu. I can have a good discussion with a Québécois, but I am not able to have a friendship with him. (male, twenties)

What happened is that when I came here, I was taught prejudices and stereotypes about the Québécois. We joked about the Québécois accent. I was told to ignore them. I was told they were woodcutters who came from the woods, and were not cultured. Unfortunately, this stereotype is still around. It took some time before I got rid of these stereotyped ideas... As soon as I had a free moment, I went to the Centre Hillel and the Québécois did not interest me. Today I work with the Québecois; I live with a Québécois woman and I am opening myself up to them. Of course there are still differences whether we like it or not—in terms of the jokes, culture and memories. But in the end, we always find common interests. I find the Québécois are very warm and very hospitable. Nonetheless, they have prejudices about the Jews that are abominable;they always have this stereotype of the greedy Jew who has money and power. (male, twenties)

Relationships with anglophones are also absent and the judgement of them by some respondents is quite direct:

> Those that I knew disgusted me. Everything is material, without scruples. I talk of the ones I work with. Everything has to do with making money. (male, twenties)

This qualitative data on social distance between Moroccan Jews and other ethnic groups confirm the quantitative data obtained by Tchorik-Pelletier (1989) in a CEGEP of the Montreal region. The data shows that the francophone Jews have relatively few contacts with the Québécois and that they maintain a greater social distance between them than with other ethnic groups.

The distance between the groups is also reflected in the importance of the Moroccan group outside school activities, in particular the Centre Hillel which serves as a rallying point for the young adults, but sometimes also as a protective cocoon, sometimes too restricted:

> The Centre Hillel has allowed me to know a lot of people, I participated in its activities, but always ignoring what was around me. I lived only with my friends, my closed group... I only lived with Moroccan Jews and I ignored the outside. (male, twenties)

> The first people I knew at Collège Français and at the Centre Hillel were Moroccans, Jews and Muslims. Overnight, I found myself bathed in a Moroccan milieu in which I had never been so embedded. For the first six months it worked very well, but soon I felt smothered. I need to say that the same people that were at the Collège went to the Centre Hillel. They would leave the Collège to meet at Hillel and would do their homework together or play ping-pong. It's a thing I always avoided doing. (female, twenties)

Mixed marriages, contrary to the mimetic generation, do not generate a lot of enthusiasm. Without being always condemned, they are nonetheless perceived by some as potential sources of conflicts and malaise:

> I do not condemn mixed marriages between Jews and Québécois; it's a choice I respect. However, I think there would be more failures because sooner or later, there are problems that can surface, especially concerning respect for tradition. You can forget them for a while, but one day or another the lid will explode and it's not going to end well. (male, twenties)

> When I become a parent I will give my children a Jewish education, because for me it's essential to one's upbringing. In any case, my choice of partner was made with that in mind. (male, twenties)

The relationship to Judaism is also perceived according to various modalities: orthodox forms coexist with respect for traditions, community commitments or a more cultural conception:

> The practice of Judaism allows me to develop my feeling of identity with the Jewish people. I really feel that I belong to this people. For me, Jewish identity is necessarily linked to religious practice. Practicing Judaism, is not simply a quest for identity or an intellectual fad. It has become a duty. (male, twenties)

> We all go to the synagogue, but I can honestly say that it is more out of respect for my father than going for myself. (male, twenties)

> We can't say that we are not Jewish, even if we do not believe in religion, even if we do not believe in God. I think it is an identity; it's beyond religion. It's a culture. (female, twenties)

Israel, which many have visited several times, constitutes an important pole of attraction. Some manifest a wish to emigrate, notwithstanding the concrete difficulties that such a departure would entail:

> Israel. I hear so much about Israel. I want to satisfy my curiosity, to travel there and to understand why everyone speaks of Israel so much. (male, twenties)
>
> I have a very complex relationship with Israel. It is ambiguous and paradoxical. For me it is essential that all Jews go to Israel. What has stopped me until now... is firstly that I started my studies. I integrated myself well into the community. There is also the financial problems of Israel. It made me think, and that put things into perspective. One thing is sure, if I have to leave Canada, it will be for Israel. I know I will emigrate to Israel one day. (male, twenties)
>
> To return to Israel, you need to have an ideal. And it's not so obvious to have such an ideal. Maybe one day, I will go to Israel, because for me, Canada is a springboard, but where to go after? At the same time, I can't imagine that I would spend the rest of my life here. Firstly because of the climate, and further, I do not feel a hundred percent integrated. I am always differentiated by my accent and my way of thinking, in fact I want to know another country where I will feel more like myself, where I will be happier. Maybe in Israel. As soon as I'll put my foot there, I feel good. Nobody will say bloody immigrant. (male, twenties)

These feelings of ambivalence are also manifested in the interviews by a lack of political interest. Many of these young people do not get involved in local or international causes, even on behalf of Jews, and their involvement in the community is essentially limited to leisure activities while cultural activities do not generate a great enthusiasm for many. On the whole, they seem to be conformist and maintain a marginal position towards the dilemmas confronting Canadian and Québécois society.

Conclusions

The analysis of the in-depth interviews done with a random sampling of Moroccan Jews belonging to different generations, has allowed us to examine their different strategies of adjustment to Montreal society. On the whole, their perception of Canada and Québec is positive. Immigration has ensured, at least for our respondents, a level of well-being and freedom that climatic conditions barely temper. As a land of immigration, Québec appears as a safe haven where it is possible to maintain one's own identity and to adapt it to surrounding conditions.

Among the older people, the problems linked to integration to the new milieu (language, work, social relations, climate), are paramount and nostalgia is dominant in their outlook. Through a mythical reconstruction of the past, associated with a golden age, they maintain values that diminish the impact of culture-shock and transplantation. By furnishing an imaginary recourse to reduce the psycho-social disorganization provoked by immigration, nostalgia functions as a buffer process which can affect the final integration to the host country.

For the middle generation, that arrived at a younger age in Québec, the relationship to the new society is mediated through the symbolic dimensions of freedom and challenge. Mimetism is the prevalent mechanism of adaptation by which the social values of the new milieu are incorporated by them into a new Moroccan Jewish identity. The development of institutional completeness, through the establishment of specific institutions and the creation or reconstitution of family and friendship networks, if not of neighborhoods, serves as a focus for community activities without inhibiting successful participation in the wider society; even if politics still means for them the internal development of the community. The third generation seems more ambivalent as to its final integration. Often isolated from the general society both by a closed school system and by the community milieu, the youngest do not fully participate, for the most part, in the contemporary debates that stir Québécois society. The relationships they have with the Québécois remain limited and superficial, marked by a lack of knowledge and interest, which contrasts, for example, with the position of the young Jews of Algerian origin living in France. Allouche-Benayoun and Bensimon note on this subject that "at university, at work, in their leisure activities and their neighborhood relationships, the Jewish youth lives among a non-Jewish majority. The barriers which, in Algeria separated the ethno-religious groups, have fallen. Therefore, mixed marriages are increasing."[9]

The politics of multiculturalism favoured in Canada have helped the maintenance of a stronger ethno-cultural identity at the expense of a real political integration into the host society. The socio-cultural pluralism of Québec seems to add itself to the factors linked to the specific variables in industrial societies as defined by Schnapper to explain the survival or the rediscovery of particularist orientations:[10]

> 1) material prosperity which allows certain lifestyles and consumer behavior to be maintained, 2) increased free time, 3) a significant increase in the general cultural level and 4) an increased motivation towards individualized self-expressions and distinctive forms of personality development in societies characterized by an industrial and bureaucratic organization of work, as well as a tendency towards a standardized consumerism.

This group of factors has amplified the tendency of the Moroccan Jewish community to maintain its specific identity, since the French colonization process happened later in Morocco than in Algeria where the Jews obtained French nationality at the end of the nineteenth century. Because of this time lag, the relative autonomy enjoyed by the Moroccan Jewish community under the system of *dhimma* (or protection) was maintained much longer in the former country. It seems that the Judeo-Moroccan group living in Montreal continues to avail itself of this perspective: to maintain its socio-cultural distinctiveness as much as possible, while adapting itself economically and ideologically to the demands of the host country, but at the expense of a deeper political involvement which still needs to be developed.

Notes

1. M. Elbaz. "D'immigrants à ethniques: analyse comparée des pratiques sociales et identitaires des Sépharades et Achkenazes de Montréal." In *Juifs du Maghreb: Diasporas contemporaines*, sous la direction de J.-C. Lasry et Claude Tapia. Paris: L'Harmattan et Presses de l'Université de Montréal, 1989, 79-102.

2. J.J. Lévy, and L. Ouaknine. "Les institutions communautaires des juifs marocains de Montréal." In *Juifs du Maghreb: Diasporas ontemporaines*, sous la direction de J.-C. Lasry et Claude Tapia. Paris: L'Harmattan et Presses de l'Université de Montréal, 1989, 55-78.

3. M. Elbaz. "D'immigrants à ethniques: analyse comparée des pratiques sociales et identitaires des Sépharades et Achkenazes de Montréal." In *Juifs du Maghreb: Diasporas contemporaines*, sous la direction de J.-C. Lasry et Claude Tapia. Paris: L'Harmattan et Presses de l'Université de Montréal, 1989, 79-102.

4. *Ibid.* J-C. Lasry. "Essor et tradition: la communauté juive nord-africaine de Montréal." In *Juifs du Maghreb: Diasporas contemporaines*, sous la direction de J.-C. Lasry et Claude Tapia. Paris: L'Harmattan et Presses de l'Université de Montréal, 1989, 15-54.

5. M. Berdugo-Cohen, Y. Cohen, and J.J. Lévy. *Juifs marocains à Montréal. Témoignages d'une immigration moderne*. Montréal: VLB éditeur, 1987.

6. The life stories had been gathered by our now deceased collaborator, Marie Berdugo-Cohen, between 1984 and 1986. She proceeded to do extensive interviews with women and men she personally knew. These biographies offer precious source material. We hope we'll be able to publish them soon.

7. J. Allouche-Benayoun, and D. Bensimon. *Juifs d'Algérie, hier et aujourd'hui*. Paris: Bibliothèque historique Privat, 1989. Benveniste. *Le Bosphore à la Roquette. La communauté judéo-espagnole à Paris (1914-1940)*. Paris: L'Harmattan, 1989. D. Schnapper. *Jewish Identities in France. An Analysis of Contemporary French Jewry*. Chicago: University of Chicago Press, 1983.

8. Elbaz, "D'immigrants à ethniques" 96.

9. J. Allouche-Benayoun, and D. Bensimon. *Juifs d'Algérie, hier et aujourd'hui*, 246.

10. D. Schnapper. *Jewish Identities in France. An Analysis of Contemporary French Jewry.*

A Female Rite of Passage in a Montreal Modern Orthodox Synagogue
The Bat Mitzvah Ceremony

SIMCHA FISHBANE

> Ritual facilitates change and it insures continuity. Throughout the ages, rituals developed to mark change from one clearly defined status, stage or place, and they functioned to maintain the community... Ritual speaks to these seeming opposites because it works at multiple levels. At one level it facilitates change in the context of the community, and at the other, it facilitates continuity while celebrating change. Through the use of symbols within the parameters of a safe structure that gives shape and direction to change, rituals work to connect the individual, the family and the larger community. Through a complex sociological and psychological process the initiate's transformation is incorporated into the community.
>
> —Judith Davis[1]

IN MY RESEARCH in the Montreal Jewish community I have been concerned with rituals or, to be more specific, rites of passage. I have argued that one goal implicitly sought through the participation and performance of Jewish rituals is to serve the needs of the community and to thereby reflect the Jewish community's zeitgeist. As Mary Douglas so beautifully put it in her discussion of death rituals, "society is ruthless in its exploitation of the bereaved to serve its own purposes."[2] As Douglas further suggests, "the analysis of ritual symbolism cannot begin until we recognize ritual as an attempt to create and maintain a particular culture, a particular set of assumptions by which experience is controlled."[3]

Although most previous studies apply the above theories of ritual and collective needs to data accumulated from primitive societies I believe it applies to contemporary Judaism.[4]

This article is an analysis of the Bat Mitzvah ritual, the rite of passage of a twelve-year-old girl,[5] as celebrated in a modern Orthodox synagogue in Montreal.

The data for this study was gathered during a two year period of participant observation.[6] In addition to attending services and religious functions of the synagogue on an ongoing basis I was involved in educational and social activities including Bar/Bat Mitzvah parties. Furthermore, twenty-five synagogue families and all professional staff were interviewed. As I am an observant Jew, I was accepted by the synagogue members as an insider. This facilitated the task of gathering data. In addition, my insider status allowed me access to the group, obtaining its trust and permission to conduct my research. There are scholars who argue that this method of gathering data is not objective, but I accept Samuel Heilman's approach to participant observation, "...as an insider I could supply, both through introspection and a sense of the relevant question to ask, information about dimensions of inner life not readily available to pure researchers."[7]

The celebration of the Bat Mitzvah ritual in the Orthodox synagogue is relatively a new phenomenon. During the first half of this century a religious ceremony for the twelve year old girl was not even considered in the North American Orthodox Judaic world. Even a birthday party with religious connotations was frowned upon. (Such birthday parties have become acceptable today even in the ultra-Orthodox Jewish community). The attitude towards Bat Mitzvah is conveyed in the writings of a major Rabbinical authority of the twentieth century, Rabbi Moshe Feinstein.[8] In a resposum dated 1957, he wrote that it should not be done in the synagogue since in the synagogue one should not perform or have activities that are not of obligatory religious significance. Rabbi Feinstein continued:

> The ceremony of Bat Mitzvah is certainly only *reshut* [non obligatory] and general vanity. There is no place to permit this [celebration] in the synagogue. Even more so as the source [of Bat Mitzvah] stems from the Reform and Conservative [Jews]. Only if the Father wants to have some type of celebration in his home is it permitted, but there is no issue here of *mitzvah* [commandment] or a *seudat* mitzvah [a meal with religious significance]. For this [celebration] is only the celebration of a birthday party.

Rabbi Feinstein then spoke against the North American style of celebrating Bar Mitzvah and continued, "But to innovate such a [celebration] with girls that is without any rabbinical source [is forbidden] it would be better to avoid [a celebration] even at home even though it is not forbidden."[9]

In 1959 Rabbi Feinstein again wrote against the idea of Bat Mitzvah though not as fervently as previously.[10] He again stated that it is not a *mitzvah*, and that a special meal should not be held in the synagogue. However, one would be allowed to have a "*kiddush.*"[11]

In 1961 Rabbi Feinstein wrote that if a hall for "parties" was originally constructed in the synagogue then it is permissible to have the Bat Mitzvah celebration in the synagogue. It seems that Rabbi Feinstein in this responsum was not as ardently against the concept as two years earlier. As we shall see, since 1961 Orthodox Rabbis have permitted themselves greater flexibility in their attitude towards the Bat Mitzvah celebration.

Social and religious pressures from the changing role of women in North American society have inspired the leadership of the Orthodox rabbinical world to reconsider and modify (without compromise to *halakhah* [Judaic law]) its position on Bat Mitzvah. The evolution of Jewish education for girls and the opening of "*yeshivot*" (schools for Judaic learning) for girls has implicitly encouraged women's greater ritual participation in Judaism.[12] It must be emphasized that though the girls aspire to greater ritual activity, such activity could not be construed to compromise *halakhah* and requires the endorsement of (male) rabbinical authorities. For the male, who throughout Jewish history has been the focus of Jewish ritual, especially where the synagogue was concerned, it was a natural process to incorporate adapt and reshape the Bar Mitzvah ritual into the existing commandments he was obligated to perform.[13] These included being called to the Torah, leading the congregation in prayer, studying and teaching Torah. It was a natural process, as I show in my paper on Bar Mitzvah,[14] for the Jewish leadership to employ this framework to serve the community's needs and thus develop the ceremony in the direction they needed. For the girl the problem was more complicated because there was no religious framework to build upon other than the Bar Mitzvah ceremony. This problem was made even more acute since it involved the synagogue, considered by many to be men's territory. This is reflected in her placement behind the *mechitza*, a barrier, wall or even separate room where the women must sit during services. But, as I suggested above, the leadership realized that it was essential due to changing educational and social realities to modify their previous stance on Bat Mitzvah. Such a modification was evident in the synagogue I observed.

The synagogue under study, which I will refer to as MZ, is a modern Orthodox synagogue located in the suburbs of Montreal. The demographic data published by the city's Jewish communal services indicate that approximately 2,000 Jewish families resided in this suburb[15] at the time of my research. The economic status of the community can be identified as middle and upper-middle class. The median age of adults identified with the synagogue is between thirty and forty-five. A family with two or three children of elementary school age is the norm.

There are eight hundred families registered as paid members of MZ synagogue. There is one other synagogue in the community which is affiliated with the reform movement and which claims a membership of seventy families. To acquire and maintain membership in MZ, a family must pay an annual membership fee of five hundred dollars. Single applicants have reduced rates. Membership allows one the right to receive priority in financial consideration and to participate in the educational, social and religious functions of the synagogue. For example, members pay substantially lower tuition fees when they enroll children in the Hebrew day-school affiliated with the synagogue. Furthermore, only a member is permitted to celebrate a Bar/Bat Mitzvah in MZ. This privilege includes the rabbi's religious instruction and guidance on matters pertaining to the ceremony, the renting of a hall and any additional organizational services related to the social functions held in the synagogue.

MZ is identified with the "left" wing of the modern Orthodox movement, which attempts to "bend" *halakhah* to its maximum, though retaining specific rituals such as the Bar Mitzvah. An example of compromise can be seen in the fact that the *halakhic* requirement for the height of the barrier that separates the sexes in the sanctuary (*mechitzah*), a barrier which in a sense defines an Orthodox synagogue, is the *halakhic* minimum. The liberalism is related to the fact that, of the eight hundred dues paying families in the synagogue, no more than fifteen identify themselves as *halakhically* observant Jews.

The synagogue is organized and functions as a corporate organization with an executive body headed by a president. It is dependent upon its members for financial support. In addition to the annual dues, revenue is generated through fund-raising functions, contributions and services provided to its members. The Bat Mitzvah celebration is one of these synagogue services.

MZ's staff is hired by the executive body. This staff includes the Rabbi, cantor, executive director, youth director and party coordinator who also officiates as the *kashruth* supervisor. Functionally, the Rabbi is the ultimate power in decision making. He is directly involved in all religious, educational, social, administrative and personnel decisions. His salary, the highest of the professional staff, is representative of his status. One of his functions is to guide, advise and instruct the Bat Mitzvah candidate in the content and role play of the Bat Mitzvah ceremony. The cantor and party coordinator, in addition to their title roles, may also assist in the instruction. The executive director is concerned with the technical and physical process in the synagogue. His functions include the technical arrangements for the Bat Mitzvah ceremony and party.

The synagogue architecture is in consonance with its members and their social allegiance. It is a modern structure with traditional Jewish symbols, pictures and artifacts. In addition to the sanctuary, chapel, reception hall and kitchen, its buildings encompass offices, two schools, meeting rooms and a Judaica artifact store. A brief description of the sanctuary is necessary to properly understand the symbolic representation of the Bat Mitzvah ritual.

The ark, containing the Torah scrolls, is situated against the eastern wall. On the northern side of the ark are positioned six "throne-like" seats. The rabbi sits closest to the ark, adjacent to the president, two sextons and the cantor. The ark and the "thrones" are positioned on a raised platform (*bimah*). On the *bimah* also is a table (*shulkhan*) where the Torah scrolls are read and the prayer leader or cantor stands. Two benches are located behind the *shulkhan* at the edge of the *bimah* farthest from the ark. On this *bimah* also stands the Bat Mitzvah girl when she delivers her address.

This design is standard in many Orthodox synagogues. MZ, in consonance with Rabbinic law requires men and women to sit separately. The *mechitzah*, a three foot barrier, separates the sexes in the MZ sanctuary. The men's section, positioned between two women's sections, is divided into three sub-sections. The middle section, directly facing the ark, is employed for the Bat Mitzvah's family and guests (males). The Bat Mitzvah girl, family and guests (female) sit on a raised section (behind the *mechitzah*) north of the *bimah*, behind the northern male sub-section. Men and women use the same entrance to enter the sanctuary. The women to, reach their seats in the northern women's section, must pass through the back rows of the men's area. This description of the sanctuary sets the stage to understand the symbolic meaning of the Bat Mitzvah ritual.

Applying anthropological theory to the ritual of Bat Mitzvah one turns to Van Gennep's[16] typology of rites of passage which is also consistent with Victor Turner's[17] understanding of the preliminal, liminal and post-liminal states that accompany the process. Van Gennep studied the order and content of the life cycle rituals in primitive societies, and characterized these periods in the individual's life as rites of passage. He indicated that to pass from one phase to another, the individual must fulfill certain conditions usually enveloped in ceremonial acts or rituals. "For every one of these events there are ceremonies whose essential purpose is to enable the individual to pass from one defined position to another which is equally well defined."[18] When crossing the order of each new stage the person is "unifying himself with a new world." Van Genepp then sub-divided each life cycle period or rite of passage into three phases; the separation from the previous status or preliminal phase, a transitional or liminal stage, and the reincorporation into a new period or post-liminal stage. A phase may not be developed to the same extent in each specific set of society's ceremonies. This tripartite structure theory has direct relevance to social change and the social consciousness of the society studied.

The Bat Mitzvah candidate at MZ begins her preparatory or separation phase approximately one half year prior to the celebration of the ritual. It must be pointed out that in this synagogue the ceremony is not termed Bat Mitzvah but rather *Bat Chachmah* (daughter or age of wisdom). The synagogue's Rabbi explained that the change in name was so that the ritual should not be a clone of the Bar Mitzvah. As to the choice of the term *chachmah* he further explains that it was chosen "since the girl shares and gains from the knowledge of Judaism." The preparation is usually directed and assigned by the rabbi. It is not uncommon that the study project is done by more than one girl and thus the celebration is a group ritual. The girl is not estranged from Jewish studies or Hebrew when she begins this project but rather must have completed at least four years of Jewish study, usually in the synagogue's Hebrew school. The beginning of the project is an announcement to her peer group as well as her family and community that she has begun to prepare for her new status and is different from the other, younger girls. She is now in the liminal stage, not yet having gone through the ritual but different from the others. In the words of Victor Turner, she is betwixt and between.

The girl's project will usually include a number of components. First a topic to be researched by the candidate must be found. It will relate to a Torah theme agreed upon by the Rabbi and the girl or girls. It is always a Jewish theme but is limited to no one specific area and is not directly related to the weekly Torah portion. Each candidate makes her own decision. Second, the girl will prepare sections of the Torah (not the weekly Torah portion) or prophets to be read from a book rather the Torah scroll. Again the fact that it is not from the weekly portion is to emphasize the fact that it is not part of the ritual Sabbath service.

The family can often choose when the ceremony will take place. They can express a preference for a Friday night, Saturday evening or Sunday celebration. The latter two are more encouraged since it involves less guests driving to synagogue on the sabbath. The Saturday night ceremony also will include participation in the *havdalah* ceremony. Here the girl is permitted to hold the candle.

Often the parents are involved in coming to the synagogue to participate in the rehearsals and follow the advancement of their daughter. Invitation lists, renting of the hall, organizing the party as well as purchasing the proper attire (non-ritualistic) for the celebration are all a family affair. Thus, as Davis correctly points out, the family during the months of preparation prior to the ceremony is implicitly trying to create a "sacred" space in which it and the child can be nurtured and cushioned through the transition. Without any doubt, it seems that the ordeal of Bar (Bat) Mitzvah is not simply the child's initiation, but a rite of passage for the entire family.[19]

The liminal stage is completed at the ceremony itself. At the actual services the girl does not participate. The father may be invited to the Torah where a special blessing will be made for his daughter. The Rabbi will devote a portion of his sermon to the Bat Mitzvah girl and her family (as he does for a Bar Mitzvah boy). Only after the services are completed will the girl's ritual commence. The Rabbi, in order to emphasize this point, explained that the men and women are then allowed to sit together to denote that it is not a prayer service.

The girl stands in the sanctuary on the *bimah*, the stage and table where the Torah is read that is situated in front of the ark that contains the Torah scrolls. Facing the guests she delivers her prepared work. At the commencement of the delivery the guests are invited to the "party." The invitation, accompanied by words of support and admiration for the girl's Jewish accomplishments, her place and family role in the Jewish community are usually spoken by the Rabbi.

The reception or festive meal does not explicitly subsume or continue the Bat Mitzvah ritual. It cannot be identified as different from other festive meals or birthday parties. It thus is almost identical to the Bar Mitzvah reception. If the party is held on the Sabbath the Rabbi will introduce general Jewish rituals such as the blessing over the wine, bread and grace after meals. If celebrated on the Sabbath no desecration of the day is permitted. At a Saturday night or Sunday reception similar religious rituals take place, but other elements such as a band, photographer and candle lighting ceremonies are incorporated. One should note that the meal, as a total entity in itself is relevant to the social consciousness of the community. Meals are an important part of most rites of passage, and their nuances have been explored in detail by social scientists. But, in each social setting, they serve different goals. The Bar/Bat Mitzvah party, in its stage and performance resembles a secular party and is therefore representative of a pluralistic society and the participants' identification with it. The difference is that it is held in the synagogue and within the framework of a religious rite. Thus the participants who attend the service and who are invited to the reception are given an opportunity to strengthen their Jewish friendship bonds and sense of belonging to the "group." If for a Jew to participate in the services requires a minimum degree of Jewish learning which might discourage some from attending, the festive meal does not. The guests do not on the whole frequent the synagogue on a regular basis, but in this setting, the service and then the meal are a proclamation, strengthening and reaffirmation of their Jewish identification. Furthermore, invitations are reciprocal, thereby allowing this process to repeat itself.

If we view the Bat Mitzvah ritual as a total structured complex composed of individual rites, we can begin to see the correlation between it and the needs of the Jewish community. Each rite serves society's collective needs. In this case the need is to foster Jewish identification. The pluralistic society of North America has contributed greatly to a large percentage of assimilation amongst the Jews. In a period when the substantive content of Jewish identity from one generation to the next is seen as in doubt,[20] a major issue confronted by Jewish leadership is Jewish identification. At the same time, the demand for participation in Jewish ritual and Jewish leadership by women has increased. My research at MZ has shown that women's role in the administration and non-religious ritual activities in the synagogue is significant. In other words the continuation and proper functioning of a Modern Orthodox Synagogue has become greatly dependent on women's participation. Moreover, the wife/mother's influence in the home in religious affairs has also become more significant. Her husband does not have the time or often even the desire to attend religious services. It is she who is now the synagogue activist. To guarantee the Bat Mitzvah girl's personal Jewish identification as well as to reaffirm the family's, girl's rites of passage could not be ignored. It is thus irrelevant if the child is treated no differently by his/her parents, teachers and peer group the next day, the experienced affirmation has enhanced everyone's connection with the Jewish community.

The Bat Mitzvah ritual, lacking its own Jewish framework to fall back upon, mirrors the Bar Mitzvah ceremony as closely as possible. In a society where most religious rituals have been abandoned it was necessary to choose ceremonies that most people could identify with. Consequently they could be used to serve the community's needs. We must perceive the synagogue, within the Jews' collective consciousness as a "micro" Jewish society.[21] This collective structure, although greatly altered in its social and religious form, has remained intact. The "synagogue," cognizant of the ethnic-national identity of the North American Jews as well as the rituals they have selected to preserve, has incorporated these elements into its collective structure and purpose.

Functioning as a corporate social structure, the synagogue sponsors social, political and educational activities that do not explicitly threaten the individuals' beliefs, but rather allow each member to choose his or her "religious expression." Thus the collective need is encouraged, developed and expressed through all the synagogue's activities and rituals whether sacred or secular. This social organization has generated rituals. The activities mould the patterns and forms manifested through the rituals which are often identified as uniquely North American. Thus the synagogue member achieves his or her religious fulfillment while the synagogue assumes the role, for many North American Jews, as the defender and preserver of Rabbinic Judaism. The Bat Mitzvah has become one ritual, even though at first rejected in the Orthodox synagogue, that demonstrates this role.

In addition, on a functional level, the Bat Mitzvah rite of passage contributes to a more dynamic and active synagogue. A larger more functional synagogue means a greater opportunity to supply the services needed to fulfill the role of defender and preserver of the borders of Rabbinic Judaism. As Durkheim notes, a stronger corporate order goes with a sense of power and potency.

The Bat Mitzvah ritual at MZ, as part of a puzzle joining neatly together to form the total picture, serves these communal needs. The Bat Mitzvah has as a prerequisite four years of Jewish education. This is considered to be basic in engendering greater commitment to Jewish identity. This commitment is further strengthened during the period of the Bat Mitzvah preparations, especially studying with the Rabbi. Greater involvement with the synagogue both in terms of physical presence as well as technical arrangements, such as the renting of the hall, caterer, etc. presumably increases the family's Jewish commitment. The family and guests coming together at the Bat Mitzvah ritual in the synagogue are further reaffirming their collective identity. This ritual practice serves to reinforce the feeling of group solidarity and to encourage, strengthen and foster attachment to the Jewish collectivity. The structured symbols, such as ritual language, music and motions of liturgy, all contribute to this communication and solidarity.

It must also be taken into consideration that the economic aspect of the Bat Mitzvah is an essential factor in the "maintenance" of the synagogue. Only members may have their daughters become *Bat Chachmah* at MZ, thus compelling families who otherwise would not join to become synagogue members. The necessary membership dues, the service charge for the hall, as well as other financial considerations that must be attended to, provide an income for the synagogue's corporate structure. The income not only contributes significantly to the maintenance of the synagogue, but also allows for development and growth. This results in a greater opportunity to serve the collective need. Thus the collective need enhances, strengthens and lays the groundwork for the maintenance of Jewish identity in the future.

To conclude I offer Jack Lightstone's insight into contemporary North American Jewry: "Jews have maintained a distinctive group identity yet fully participate in the large social milieu, because of the particular structure of myth, symbol and ritual which by consensus has developed and furnished a new Jewish identity."[22]

Notes

1. Judith Davis, "The Bar Mitzvah as a Multigenerational Ritual of Change and Continuity," in *Essays in the Social Scientific Study of Judaism and Jewish Society,* S. Fishbane and J. Lightstone editors. Montreal: Concordia University, 1990.

2. Mary Douglas, *Cultural Bias.* London: Royal Anthropological Institute of Great Britian and Ireland, 1979.

3. Mary Douglas, *Purity and Danger.* London: Ark Paperbacks, 1966.

4. For an example of this discussion see Samuel Heilman, *Defenders of the Faith*. New York: Schocken Books, 1992, XVII-XVIII.

5. While the Bar Mitzvah ritual for the boy in an initiation into the adult society, the reaching of twelve years for the girl was without ceremony.

6. A full description of this participant observation is in my article "Contemporary Bar Mitzvah Rituals in Modern Orthodoxy," *Journal of Religion and Culture* 2 (1987).

7. Heilman, *Synagogue Life,* Chicago, University of Chicago Press, 1973, xi. Although Heilman suggests in a later writing (*Defenders of the Faith*) differently I accept his original hypothesis.

8. An interesting description of Rabbi Feinstein's attitude towards women can be found in Norma Joseph, "The Traditional Denial of Change: Women's Place in the World of Rabbi Moses Feinstein" in *Journal of Religion and Culture*, Volume 2 Number 1, (Fall, 1983)

9. *Orakh Chaim* volume 1, responsum 104.

10. *Orakh Chaim* volume 6 responsum 36.

11. Refreshments after the prayer that borders on a party depending on its extravagance.

12. For a discussion on education for girls with bibliographical sources see Heilman, *Defenders of the Faith* pages 35, n. 74; 173, n. 11.

13. As Claude Levi-Strauss describes culture it is "the interweaving of cultural threads from different arenas," *Tristes Tropiques*, trans. John and Doreen Weightman. New York: Washington Square Press, 1973, 9.

14. Simcha Fishbane, "Contemporary Bar Mitzvah Rituals in Modern Orthodoxy," in *Journal of Religion and Culture*, Volume 2 Number 1 Fall, 1987.

15. Since the time that the data for this study was gathered the demographic data has changed. The changes bear little relevance upon the results of this work.

16. Van Gennep A. *The Rites of Passage*. Chicago: The University of Chicago Press, 1960.

17. Victor Turner, *The Ritual Process: Structure and Antistructure*. Chicago: Aldine Publishing, 1969.

18. Ibid.

19. Judith Davis, "The Bar Mitzvah as a Multigenerational Ritual of Change and Continuity," in *Essays in the Social Scientific Study of Judaism and Jewish Society*, S. Fishbane and J. Lightstone editors, Concordia University, 1990.

20. Stuart Schoenfeld, "Some Aspects of the Social Significance of Bar/Bat Mitzvah Celebration" in *Essays in the Social Scientific Study of Judaism and Jewish Society*, S. Fishbane and J. Lightstone editors. Montreal: Concordia University, 1990.

21. Simcha Fishbane, "Contemporary Bar Mitzvah Rituals in Modern Orthodoxy," in *Journal of Religion and Culture* , Volume 2 Number 1 Fall, 1987.

22. Cited in Fishbane "Contemporary Bar Mitzvah Rituals," 186.

A.M. Klein's *The Rocking Chair*
A Re-Vision of Québec

RACHEL FELDHAY BRENNER

A.M. KLEIN'S LAST BOOK of poetry was published in 1948. *The Rocking Chair and Other Poems*[1] which focuses on the province of Québec has been appraised as Klein's best poetic achievement. Some critics focused on the Jewish poet's deliberate immersion into the French Canadian environment.[2] Others portrayed Klein's treatment of Québec as a representation of the humanist ideal which transcends ethnic differentiations.[3] Still others wished to highlight Klein's attraction to Christian symbolism.[4]

These readings of *The Rocking Chair* concur with Klein's own explicitly ideological statement concerning his "Québec poetry." In an introductory letter to the poems, Klein explained that he had decided to "look upon the French Canadian" because

> we have many things in common: a minority position; ancient memories; and a desire for group survival. Moreover the French Canadian enjoys much—a continuing and distinctive culture, solidarity, land—which I would wish on my people.[5]

To enclose a literary text within the parameters of an ideological agenda, even the author's own, turns it into a finalized product rather than a source of dynamic exchange between the author and the reader. The ideologically oriented interpretation canonizes the text turning it into a spokespiece of its interpreters.[6]

It seems that Klein's selection and organization of the volume questions its declared intentionality as the vehicle of humanist trust in the fellowship of humankind. D.H. Lawrence's famous dictum "Never trust the artist. Trust the tale," seems a useful reminder that the complex voice of art often refutes ideological simplifications.

Indeed, Klein's "Québec Poems" emit voices which belie its critical appreciation as a statement of humanistic benevolence. As the volume unfolds, its tone becomes increasingly satirical and embittered. In the final ten poems, not even one offers a promise of a brighter future in the reality of unrelieved social inequality, materialism and bigotry. In general, the optimistic poems which carry the humanistic message are few, clustered mainly in the beginning of the volume; in the mid-section a few lyrical poems about Montreal commemorate the city as the idyllic site of the poet's idealized childhood.

The final poem, "Portrait of the Poet as Landscape," as the signature of the volume generates the most pertinent doubt about the "humanist" reading of *The Rocking Chair*. In fact, the poem represents authorial self-elimination from the text. It starts with a series of negative statements:

> Not an editorial-writer...
> mourns him, the *shelved Lycidas*.
> No actress squeezes a glycerine tear for him.
> The radio broadcast lets his passing pass.
> And with the police, no record. Nobody,
>   it appears,
> ...missed him enough to report. (331)

The poem ends with a startling image of the drowned poet:

> ...he [the poet]
> makes of his status as zero a rich garland,
> a halo of his *anonymity*,
> and lives alone, and in his secret shines
> like phosphorus. At the bottom of the sea. (335)

It seems of crucial importance that the volume ends with a world picture in which the "lost" poet sings of his effacement. The abstraction of the poet's anonymity invalidates the critical interpretation of humanistic optimism and presents the text as the poet's reckoning with the meaninglessness of poetry in today's world.

The poem begins by staking out its intertextual territory from James Joyce to John Milton. Klein's choice of the two great English writers is by no means incidental. Klein was an ardent Joycean scholar and a dedicated student of English poetry. The relevance of Milton merges in Klein's other works, such as *The Hitleriad* and *The Second Scroll.* Here, the poem's title "Portrait of the Poet as Landscape" reechoes Joyce's *A Portrait of the Artist as a Young Man*, while the image of "the shelved Lycidas" in the second line refers us to Milton's famous monody.

The allusions to Joyce and Milton bring forth the mythological intertexts of Icarus and Orpheus, the drowned artists who have become the emblems of man's intrinsic desire for beauty and perfection. Traditionally, the poet is an outstanding member of society, since he embodies the centrality of art in social discourse. Though the poet's song may be tragically severed and the birth of poetic vision may require painful sacrifices, neither Milton nor Joyce questions the supreme value of art in society.

Klein's intertextual construct thus focuses on the ages-old poet's self-image as the creator of civilization and culture. As a descendant of Orpheus and Icarus, the artist imparts a universal, timeless truth. However, Klein's parodic rewriting of Joyce and Milton de-mythologizes the poet's elevated social status.

In contrast with Milton's Lycidas, "the Genius of the shore" (363), and Joyce's Stephen who will "forge in the smithy of [his] soul the uncreated conscience of [his] race," (253), Klein's poet "see[s] himself as throwback, relic, freak" cheated out of his role and position (331-332). As Klein sees it, other social figures have replaced him as guides and teachers of humanity: the tycoon, the politician, the rich popular artist, the scientist and his deadly inventions (334). In contrast with the traditional view of its universality, poetry has become subject to relativism, determined by historical evolution and social change. The poet, the selected enunciator of the universal truth, has been reduced to what Klein ironically calls "a number, an x" in "our real society" (331).

The poet thus experiences a split between his "poetic" self and his "social" self. His split identity has inflicted a psychological injury manifest in the desire to restore wholeness which has been irrevocable lost. The sexual allusions in Klein's description of the poet's lost oneness with the language highlight the intensity of his vocation as a poet:

> Then he will remember his travels
> over that body—
> the torso verb, the beautiful face of the noun,
> and all those shaped and warm auxiliaries!
> A first love it was, the recognition
> of his own.
> ...
> And then remember how this made a change in him
> affecting for always the glow and growth of
> his being... (332)

The poet's conjunction with the language becomes the moment of conception, of planting a new life:

> Therefore he seeds *illusions* ... he is
> the nth Adam taking a green inventory
> in world but scarcely uttered, naming,
> praising,
> ...
> Until it has been praised, that part
> has not been. Item by exciting item-
> air to his lungs, and pressured blood to
> his heart—
> they are pulsated, and breathed,
> until they map,
> not the world's, but his own body's chart! (334-35)

Klein's poet, a divine maker who recreates the world with the breath of his word, reechoes Stephen Dedalus' vision of "the artist forging anew ... out of the sluggish matter of the earth a new soaring impalpable imperishable being ..." (169). At the same time, Klein's depiction of the poetic act as "illusions" questions the concept of poetry as an imitation of the divine act of creation. The ironic gap between the awareness of the illusory nature of poetry and the poet's passionate, physical sense of affinity with the language outlines a dramatic shift in the poetic function in today's reality. If the world regenerated through the poetic act leaves no imprint on every day existence, then the notion of the poet's indispensability to the world no longer makes sense. Klein's concluding description of the poet reduces him to a mock saint whose "status as zero" becomes "a halo of his anonymity" (335). An ignored outsider, the poet must redefine his function in a society which has lost interest in an inspired guide of humanity.

The world, then, continues to both inspire and preoccupy the poet. The purpose of this interest, however, has been transformed. Now the poet explores a world which has banished poetry. Klein's poet, positioned on the outside, examines and records the text of an artless world:

> And now in imagination he has climbed
> another planet, the better to look
> with single camera view upon this earth—
> its total scope, and each afflated tick,
> its talk, its trick, its tracklessness—
> and this,
> this, he would like to write down in
> a book! (335)

It is no longer Milton's Lycidas, the poet-saint, who affirms eternity in art; neither is it Joyce's Stephen, the poet-rebel, who wishes to recreate the human race through art. Klein's is the invisible poet whose isolated position informs his parodic self-image of a spy from outer space, surreptitiously documenting the foibles, triviality, and purposelessness of the earth's inhabitants. His images portray a world which has lost its sense of purpose.

The poem which proposes to write a book composed of the poet's observations of the world has, in fact, been placed at the conclusion of such an attempt: the text of *The Rocking Chair*—seemingly random collection of poetic vignettes—actualizes the poet's desire

> To find a new function for the déclassé craft
> archaic like the fletcher's; make a new thing;
> to say the word that will become sixth sense;
> perhaps by necessity and indirection bring
> *new force to life*, *anonymously*, new creeds... (335)

The poets must remain anonymous in a society which refuses to see him as a visionary. He represents knowledge and truth that the world would prefer to obliterate altogether.

At the psychological level, forgetfulness reaffirms the existence of the ignored object. Thus, by declaring his intention to bring new creeds by "necessity and indirection," recognition. The book about the world which "forgot" poetry confronts the world with its own suppressed consciousness.

By writing the poet out, the world, paradoxically, writes its anonymous poet in as its "sixth sense," its ignored self-knowledge. Klein's notion of the excluded poet calls into question Northrop Frye's definition of the ironic protagonist as the excluded individual, "no more deserving of what happens to him than anyone else would" (41). Here exclusion has defined the poet as his society's unconscious. He is the image and the recorder of the world's suppressed emotional landscape and as such he "...lives alone, and in his secret shines/like phosphorus. At the bottom of the sea." (335)

"Portrait of the Poet as Landscape" thus elucidates *The Rocking Chair* as an evolving metaphoric quest: in that sense, it is a text which explores and exposes the "forgotten" layers of social consciousness. Under the poet's scrutinizing lenses, Québec becomes the metonomy of the world which has estranged itself from its poetic self. The poet, unobtrusively and "by indirection," achieves his end: the intrigued readers review the text to confront the truth that they have chosen to forget.

The poems "Air-Map" and "Break-Up" outline the scope of Klein's spacial insights gained from his position of an outsider. In "Air-Map" Klein explodes Québec's illusion of innocence:

> How private and comfortable it once was,
> our white mansard beneath the continent's
> gables!
> But now, evicted, and still there-
> a wind blew off the roof?
> we see our fears and our featherbeds
> plumped white
> on the world's crossroads. (310)

The poet identifies with the pain of destroyed intimacy which has eliminated the sense of communal togetherness. Clinging to tradition can no longer whitewash anxieties and fears breaking through the facade of complacency and self-deceit. From his vantage position of a secret observer, he notes his community's unrelieved unhappiness and disorientation.

In the poem "Break-Up" the malaise of suppressed desperation ironizes the notion of natural revival. This time from his under-water post, the poet views the city's concealed anguish which transforms the hope of spring into the reality of despair:

> But it [the break-up] will come!
> ...
> [it] will melt its muscle-bound tides
> and raise from their iced tomb
> the pyramid fish, the unlockered ships,
> and last year's blue and bloated suicides. (314)

The outer-space and under-water standpoints establish the poet as a distanced observer of society. The poet's encompassing and penetrating "camera" vision of the world implies the seriousness of the social theme. As their titles indicate, the poems "map out" the "break-up" of traditions sanctified by the seemingly immutable social order.

Assuming the voice of his community's unconscious, the poet places the province of Québec on the plane of the collective psyche. Using the example of Québec, *The Rocking Chair* tells about the disintegration of culture and tradition in a reality typified by growing self-centredness, materialism, and hypocrisy.

The associative, rather than analogical or chronological, concept of arrangement foregrounds an ambivalent attitude toward both past and present. Neither the idealization of the past, nor the ruthless efficiency of the present provides the desired social model: the ingenuousness of the traditional way of life highlights the mendacity of social interrelationships today; at the same time, the increasing alienation of the individual exposes the growing ineffectuality of tradition as a unifying social factor.

The notion of a reality whose past and present parody each other is perhaps best represented in the contrastive social pictures placed each at an end of the text. They are the title poem, "The Rocking Chair," and the penultimate poem, "Annual Banquet: Chambre de Commerce." "The Rocking Chair" glorifies the unchanging rhythm of tradition. The significance of the rocking chair is emphatically spelled out; it "is tradition." It is act/ and symbol, symbol of this static folk... (296). The sense of strong national identity emerges in the final association of the rocking chair with "some Anjou ballad." The consciousness of the ancestral French origins evokes nostalgic longing for the past, solidifying the sense of ethnic identity in the recollection of the land of origin as "a first love." (296).

The placement of the poem "Annual Banquet: Chambre de Commerce" at the conclusion of the volume does not seem arbitrary. The final vision of Quebec in the volume presents a parodic transformation of the initial vision in "The Rocking Chair." Here "business time" measured by annual social events, undercuts the notion of "life time" measured by the eternal cycles of youth, maturity, and old age. The perspective of the province as an object of financial gain parodies its traditional, unworldly life style as an easy prey of exploitation by the corporate world:

Québec: The place for industry
Cheap power. Cheap labour.
No taxes (first three years).
No isms (forever). (330)

This perception of the mainstays of Québec's traditional rich family life turns it into an economic force which makes the province an attractive investment area. Ironically, the loving family relationships in "The Rocking Chair" contribute to the weakening of the community. As presented in "Annual Banquet," "love which moves the stars and factories," produces cheap labour and engenders alienation rather than a sense of unifying communal tradition.

With the disintegration of tradition, comes the decline of the poetic-prophetic stature. The juxtaposition of the two poems, "The Rocking Chair" and "Annual Banquet" exposes not only a world in transition, but the increasing social dysfunction of the poet. The disparity between the completeness and clarity of the language in "The Rocking Chair" and the fragmented, italicized journalese in "Annual Banquet" marks the poet's growing uncertainty and disillusion. The discourse between the poet and society breaks up in a reality which has rendered tradition meaningless.

The constantly reappearing motif of exploitation communicates the discrepancy between the idealized past and the corrupt present. The poem "The Grain Elevator" paints a magnificent picture of the Canadian prairie as the world's bread basket. Here bread is portrayed as the archetypal common denominator for "all the coloured faces of mankind," and the prairie, "rolled like a rug of a thick gold and golden thread," (301) promises to both nourish and nurture humankind. This image of wheat as a treasure shared by humanity is subverted in the poem "The Spinning Wheel" where the golden wheat is portrayed as the object of greed and the root of oppression of the Québec farmer by today's "incorporate seigneur." (309)

Exploitation, the manipulation of one's fellow-men for economic profit or political gain, is the decisive factor in the destruction of the humanist ideal. Contrary to the critical appreciation of *The Rocking Chair* as a programmatic humanist text, the image that emerges is that of deceit and greed for power which undermine the humanist foundations of equality and tolerance.

The poem, "Political Meeting," ironically dedicated to Camillien Houde, who fought against conscription during World War II,[7] depicts political manipulation of Québec's racist intolerance. Hatred of English Canadians is instigated through skillful demagogic exploitation of the values which structure the backbone of French Canadian tradition; the French Major

> praises the virtue of being *Canadien*,
> of being at peace, of faith, of family,
> and suddenly his other voice:
> *Where are your sons?*
> ...
> The whole street wears one face,
> shadowed and grim; and in the darkness rises
> the body-odour of race. (307-308)

As an outsider, all the poet can do is observe and denounce the ways in which basic human moral values are abused by such racists as Houde and such anti-Semitic hate mongers, as Adrien Arcand, an ardent supporter of Hitler and the leader of Québec's fascist movement. The voice of suppressed conscience which the world does not want to hear emerges in an ironic address to Arcand:

> *Et, pour vrai dire,* what more political
> is there to say after you have said:
> *A bas les maudits Juifs!* (p. 328)

The poet, however, does not dwell on injustice committed in particular against his own ethnic group; grieving the collapse of the humanist ideal, he identifies his own plight with another poignant instance of ethnic persecution. In the poem "Indian Reservation: Caughnawaga," Klein deplores the destruction of the Indian culture and tradition:

This is a grassy ghetto, and no home.
And these are fauna in a *museum* kept.
The better hunters have prevailed. The game,
losing its blood, now makes these grounds
its *crypt*. (304-305, italics mine)

It is important to note the similarity of imagery in the poem "Meditations Upon Survival," Klein's probably most profound response to the Holocaust. Here, in almost identical terms the poet mourns his own lifelessness in the wake of Jewish destruction. He sees himself as

one who, though watched and isolate, does go—
the last point of a diminished race—
the way of the *fletched buffalo*.
What else, therefore, to do
but leave these bones that are not ash to fill—
O not my father's vault—but the glass-case
some proud *museum* catalogues *Last Jew*.
(Klein 289, italics mine)

The interrelating imagery in the two poems outlines the common fate of people whose cultural distinctness has been destroyed in an act of dehumanization. Klein's poetic vision highlights the motif of reification and therefore the end of the humanist ideal. The desire to destroy peoples and their traditions in a ruthless, hateful pursuit of profit and power has reduced the "others" to lifeless artifacts.

An example of a world united in the very recognition of cultural diversity emerges in the poem "Montreal." The passionate, sweeping variety of languages and nationalities interfuse, yet remain distinct, in a metaphoric vision of the metropolis as an embodiment of the humanist ideal. For a moment, the poet seems to regain his stature of an inspired teacher of humanity conjuring up a vision of multi-racial social intercourse. Here, the Indian, the English, and the French are "all present" in the city's past, all equally [populating] the pupils of [the poet's] eyes: the proud Indian "with tabac of [his] peace enfumes the air;" the adventurous *coureur de bois* with his pelts and the dignified seigneur "within his candled manoir;" the resourceful "Scot/Ambulant through his bank" (316). And the Jewish poet unites them all in his poetry; he is the bard and troubadour who unifies its diverse languages in the music of his song:

You are a part of me, O all your quartiers—
And of dire pauvreté and of richesse—
To finished time my homage loyal claim;
You are locale of infancy, milieu
Vital of institutes that formed my fate;
And you above the city, scintillant,
Mount Royal, are my spirit's mother,
Almative, poitrinate! (317)

Klein's sense of bonding with the city is extremely powerful. In the poem, "The Mountain," the landscape blends the poet's formative experience with the universal experience of humanity at large:

> In layers of mountains the history of mankind,
> and in Mount Royal
> which daily in a street-car I surround
> my youth, my childhood... (320)

In these nostalgic reminiscences of childhood, the city emerges as the archetypal mother figure which unifies and supports in love. The image of the city's motherly solicitude reemerges in the poem "For the Sisters of the Hotel Dieu," an expression of gratitude to the motherly nuns, who took care of Klein in sickness when he was a child. Many years later, the Jewish poet, drawing upon the Franciscan bird symbol of loving-kindness, commemorates the nuns in his song of praise. At the same time, his preoccupation with humanity compels him to explore the emotional framework which makes a selfless act of love possible. As he sees it, the solicitude extended to the Jewish boy is deeply rooted in a sense of emotional wholeness in the nuns' social situation; it is the deep sense of security and togetherness that enables them to devote themselves to others:

> In pairs,
> as if to illustrate their sisterhood,
> the sisters pace the hospital garden walks.
> In their robes black and white immaculate hoods
> they are like birds... (300)

Paradoxically, the exuberance which pervades Klein's recollections of his childhood experience of the city and its inhabitants underscores the tenuousness of the humanist dream. The implausible quality of these idyllic images emerges in an ironic contrast with the book's dominant theme of alienation and exploitation. Indeed, the picture of mutually enriching relationships is proven void of meaning in one of the concluding poems, "Les Filles Majeures." The initial image of togetherness, almost identical to that of the nuns, is instantly twisted into an emblematic representation of social isolation:

> Evenings, they walk arm in arm, in pairs,
> as if to emphasize their incompleteness,
> and friendly together make an ambiguous form,
> like a folded loneliness,
> or like mirrors that reflect only each other. (328)

Whereas the nuns' sameness corroborates the distinct social function that they fulfill, the sisters lose identity in the self-perpetuating cycles of alikeness. Cut off from meaningful social roles, they circulate in the orbit of enforced alienation and sterility.

The association with the nuns in the context of "Filles" heightens the notion of purposelessness and isolation. The poignant, quiet desperation of the sisters, identical in their social exclusion, supersedes the idyllic memory of the saintly nuns. The pictures of past fulfillment trigger off the notion of present dissatisfaction, whereas the increasing sense of fragmentation in the concluding poems intensifies against the earlier representations of the happier past.

Klein's manipulation of similar images bound together in a network of associations reveals the "nervousness" of the text. The similar, but differently treated images reflect the poet's vacillations between the desire to regress to the traditional poetic act of "praising the world" and the intensifying realization of the new poetic function to explore the world which has denounced poetry. The concluding stanza of "Les Filles Majeures" extends an associative thread to the signature poem "Portrait," manifesting the poet's identification with the sterility which pervades the sisters' world:

> For them, for them the world lacks symmetry!
> And they themselves seem to themselves
> like vases broken in half,
> the halves perversely
> stood upon shelves
> unfinished, and rich with flowers never to be. (329)

The broken, shelved vases, an image of the unfulfilled promise of motherhood, invoke the poet's self-image as "the shelved Lycidas." The empty, meaningless world of spinsterhood, therefore, becomes a metaphoric representation of spiritually and culturally depleted rigid society which dooms to loneliness and despair those who do not conform. The unloved and the excluded cannot possibly create life or art, since both life and art must be conceived in a sense of wholeness and acceptance.

The poet knows why he has been socially rejected. The function of the poet as the teacher of humanity has been usurped by a new visionary: the notary has become "the true poet functional of this place" (324). Indeed, in the poem entitled "The Notary," Klein presents the image of the new ruler of society whose beliefs, customs, and life style have become subject to contractual arrangements. The poetry that permeates and shapes society today is the text of the legal document. In that sense, the notary has become the poet, renaming the world through the language of his legalistic craft.

In "Portrait," the forgotten poet dreams about renewing his poetic function by bringing "new forms to life." The parodic transformation of this dream has been realized by the notary, the poet's grotesque double. “The Notary,” as one of the most poignant insights into social interrelations confronts society with a picture of its ethical and aesthetic deterioration. The new forms that the notary brings to life underscore the lifelessness of today’s existence where even love is governed by money. These new forms of art emerge once the discourse of artists such as Milton and Joyce has been expunged. The manipulative legal contract, the racist political oratory, the profit-oriented business talk are such new language forms which shape and articulate today’s existence.

The “new function” of poetry seems to materialize in its interpretation of new social edifices erected upon the discarded ideals of the past. Perhaps the most extreme illustration of today’s social landscape emerges in the poem “Pawnshop.” The emblem of society as the house of death, the pawnshop portrays the individual as the architect of his or her own spiritual demise. The pawnshop is also the burial place of culture, religion, and ethics; it turns the world into a moral waste land:

> This is our era’s state-fair parthenon,
> the pyramid of a pharaonic time,
> our little cathedral, our platonic cave,
> our childhood’s house that Jack built. Synonym
> of all building, our house, it owns us; even
> when free from it, our dialectic grave.
> . . .
> Our own gomorrah house,
> the sodom that merely to look at
> makes one salt? (312)

Like the biblical Lot, the poet has been excluded from his immoral environment, and like Lot’s wife, he looks back from his solitary post at the city which raised him and then rejected him. Unlike Sodom and Gomorrah, however, the poet’s city is not burning; in its perpetuating sinfulness and corruption, it still waits to be redeemed. The poet can no longer assume the role of a prophetic social reformer; neither can he continue to sing in praise of human beings who have abused humanism. The unheeded poet can strive for no more than an "air-map" to outline mankind's "break-up" of humanistic values, or for an occasional in-depth glimpse of the repressed social consciousness.

As a quest for the poet's self-redefinition in face of the moral collapse of today's world, the portrayal of Quebec in *The Rocking Chair* vacillates between the idealized fantasy of the past and the satiric vision of the present. The text comes to life in the acknowledgement of its own anxiety, "nervousness," and disorientation. Indeed, the poetic exploration of poetry's vulnerability amounts to a new function of the "déclassé craft:" The poet's multiple voices searching to penetrate social obtuseness confront the world's consciousness with the suppressed voice of humanistic creed.

Notes

1. The references to *The Rocking Chair and Other Poems* are from *The Collected Poems of A.M. Klein*. Toronto: McGraw-Hill Ryerson, 1974.

2. See Sutherland 62-65; Dudek 72-73; Wilson 93.

3. See Waddington 133; Marshall xiii; Matthews 146; Bentley *ECW*, *JCS*.

4. Marya Fiamengo, 70.

5. See Caplan, 149.

6. Linda Luft Ferguson subscribes to Klein's rationale, suggesting that Klein's portrait of his province...represents a remarkable empathy, a projection of his own culture, rather than a concentrated effort to understand the culture of Quebec per se" (58).

7. See Caplan, 82.

Works Cited

Bentley, D.M.R. "A Nightmare Ordered: A.M. Klein's 'Portrait of the Poet as Landscape.'" *Essays on Canadian Writing* 28 (1994): 1-46. (*ECW*)

——. "Klein, Montreal, and Mankind." *Journal of Canadian Studies* 19.2 (1984): 34-58. (*JCS*)

Caplan, Usher. *Like One That Dreamed: A Portrait of A.M. Klein.* Toronto: McGraw-Hill Ryerson, 1982.

Dudek, Louis. "A.M. Klein." *A.M. Klein*. Ed. Tom Marshall, Toronto: The

Ryerson Press 1970, 66-74.
Ferguson, Linda Luft. "*The Rocking Chair*: Portrait of the Poet as Province." *Journal of Canadian Studies* 19.2 (1984): 58-66.
Fiamengo, Marya. "Catholic Resonances in the Poetry of A.M. Klein." *The A.M. Klein Symposium*. Ed. Seymour Mayne. Ottawa: University of Ottawa Press, 1975.65-73.
Joyce, James. *A Portrait of the Artist as a Young Man*. Harmondsworth: Penguin Books, 1966.
Klein, A.M. *The Rocking Chair and Other Poems* in *The Collected Poems of A.M. Klein*. Ed. Miriam Waddington, Toronto: McGraw-Hill Ryerson 1974.
Marshall, Tom. "Introduction." *A.M. Klein*. Ed. Tom Marshall, Toronto: The Ryerson Press 1970, vi-xxiii.
Matthews, John. "A.M. Klein." *A.M. Klein*. Ed. Tom Marshall, Toronto: The Ryerson Press 1970, 132-150.
Milton, John. *Paradise Lost and Selected Poetry and Prose*. New York: Rinehart & Co. 1951.
Sutherland, John. "Canadian Comment." *A.M. Klein*. Ed. Tom Marshall, Toronto: The Ryerson Press 1970, 59-65.
Waddington, Miriam. *A.M. Klein*. Vancouver: The Copp Clark Publishing Company, 1970.
Wilson, Milton. "Klein's Drowned Poet: Canadian Variations on an Old Theme." *A.M. Klein*. Ed. Tom Marshall, Toronto: The Ryerson Press 1970, 92-98.

The Politics of (Dis)Integration
Montreal Jewish Fiction in English

MICHAEL BENAZON

MONTREAL JEWISH WRITING is today a topic of rather vast proportions. To bring some order into the subject, it will be necessary to restrict it—firstly to post-war writing, secondly to fiction, and thirdly to works written in English. In an essay which focuses on the politics of integration, there will be a few writers whose work is not pertinent to the topic. On the other hand, Montreal writers who are no longer permanent residents of the city, together with a number of writers whose names are not well known to the reading public, will be considered.

I am not, of course, attempting to equate the talents of the authors. Some have an international following, while others may never go beyond their own time and place. I have included the work of several of the lesser known writers, because they make a valid contribution to the collectivity we call Montreal Jewish fiction, and because most of them, it seems to me, are preoccupied with the theme I shall call ambiguous integration.

It is quite possible that a number of the authors under consideration would object to being categorized as Jewish writers because, so it may seem to them, a Jewish writer is perceived as one who has a limited range and a correspondingly small audience. We may remember, for example, Mordecai Richler's original antipathy to being labelled Canadian, as if we were accusing him of not being up to international standards. While it is possible to sympathize with the reluctance of writers to be labelled, critics will inevitably be on the lookout for terms that convey meaning to their readers. So in this study, a "Montreal Jewish writer" is one who considers him\herself to be Jewish and who at times sets the action of his\her work in Montreal. This term does not imply that the writer deals only with Jewish subjects or that the audience is in any way restricted to a particular group.

Within our lifetime many of us have witnessed the flowering of a Canadian literature which we can read with genuine pleasure and concern because of what it tells us about ourselves. In recent years we have become aware of the existence of regional literatures in Canada. If it is legitimate to discuss prairie fiction, Quebec fiction, or even Montreal fiction, then it is surely legitimate to discuss Montreal Jewish fiction which, as we know, has dominated Canadian Jewish literature since World War II.

Though not a Montrealer by birth, education, or residence, I find the subject endlessly fascinating because it focuses on problems which have been, and still are, meaningful to me as a member of the Canadian Jewish community, and I assume that the topic can interest members of other minority groups in this country. Since we in Canada are all members of one minority or another, the issues raised by the Montreal Jewish prose writers should be of concern to everybody. It has been argued by Michael Greenstein and others, that the figure of the Jew, far from being peripheral to western civilization, has come to occupy a central place in the imagination because the themes of alienation, strangerhood, displacement, marginality, group loyalties, and assimilation versus integration—present in the literature—are central to our concerns everywhere in the western world today.

Having justified, I hope, my choice of topic, allow me to explain the starting point of my hypothesis. Without going into all the criticism that has been written on Montreal Jewish literature, I wish to refer to three notable essays. In his 1968 study of the Montreal novel from 1941 to 1966, Antoine Sirois argued that there were in effect not two but three distinct literary communities in Montreal—French, English, and Jewish. Sirois focuses on the French writers. He mentions only three Jewish writers—Mordecai Richler, Leonard Cohen, and Monique Bosco—and argues that in their devotion to family values and cultural identity, the Jewish novelists are akin to the Québécois novelists.

In her 1967 Master's thesis entitled "The City of Montreal in the French Canadian Novel of 1945-65," Barbara Godard also acknowledged the three-fold division in Montreal fiction. Although six Jewish writers—Richler, Cohen, C.J. Newman, William Weintraub, Herman Buller and Dr. Abram Stilman—are listed in her bibliography, she declined to discuss them in detail because, as she explains in her thesis resumé: "leurs centres d'intérêts se sont révélés différents de ceux des deux autres groupes." In her later article, "The Geography of Separatism" published in 1976 (*Laurentian University Review* 9.1), based on her Master's thesis, Professor Godard again declined to be drawn into a discussion of the Montreal Jewish novelists. She found the Montreal novel to be subtly political, with the Two Solitudes as the central theme.

The validity of the comments made by Sirois and Godard on Montreal Jewish fiction were in effect called into question by Eli Mandel in a talk he gave in December 1976 entitled "The Fabled City: Themes of Exile and Return in Canadian Jewish Writing." At that time, Mandel argued against the concept of a distinctive Jewish-Canadian literature. Paraphrasing the American critic Irving Howe, Mandel claimed that the golden age of Jewish North American writers had long since passed, that its vitality was fast fading, and that Jewish writing was beginning to disappear.

From the vantage point of 1992, it would seem that Mandel's report on the demise of Jewish-Canadian literature was, as they say, greatly exaggerated. In so far as Montreal is concerned, some of the older surviving Jewish writers—Irving Layton, Ted Allan (who died in summer 1995), Oscar Ryan, Mordecai Richler—have had a renewed burst of creativity since 1976, and their ranks have been reinforced by a considerable group of younger men and women. It is possible at this time to survey the essential characteristics of post-war Montreal Jewish fiction based on the work of roughly twenty-five writers, several of whom have by now published a substantial body of work. Though Mandel's pessimistic prediction have not materialized, his perception of a decline in the quality of the Jewishness in their writing is probably correct; I shall return to this point at the end of my essay.

Both Sirois and Godard reveal an awareness of sociological and political themes underlying the work of many Montreal novelists. They claim that French-English tensions are at the heart of much of this literature. Taking their arguments one step further, I would note that the French-language novelists present characters who resist assimilation into English-Canadian culture. The origin of this stance can no doubt be traced back to the Quebec regional novelists of the nineteenth and early twentieth centuries—Philippe-Joseph Aubert de Gaspé, Tardivel, Gérin-Lajoie, Hémon, Savard, Groulx, Ringuet—writers who express a hostility to English political, social, and economic influence. This theme remains strong in French Montreal literature, probably because Montreal is the place where assimilating pressures are most in evidence. Attacks on English economic and social power are readily found in such recent French Montreal novelists as Yves Beauchemin, Victor-Lévy Beaulieu, Roch Carrier, and older writers like Jacques Ferron and Gabrielle Roy. By and large, there can be no fraternization with the English oppressor. In *Le Couteau sur la table* and *Trou de mémoire*, novels written by Jacques Godbout and Hubert Aquin, French-Canadian protagonists murder their English-Canadian girlfriends. The English presence, however attractive, must be repudiated.

The Montreal English novelists, on the other hand, naively even wistfully look for ways to bring differing cultures together through marriage which, I would argue, can best be understood as an unconscious attempt to assimilate the other, whether it be French or Jewish, into the English cultural mainstream. We find intermarriage used as plot resolution as early as 1864 when Antoinette de Mirecourt, the heroine of Rosanna Leprohon's novel of that name, marries an English army officer. Intermarriage as a symbolic resolution of political conflict and cultural difference is a prominent motif in the work of Hugh MacLennan—*Two Solitudes* and *Return of the Sphinx* for example—as it is in Keith Henderson's more recently published *Restoration*, where the tensions engendered by the referendum debate of 1980 are allayed, if not wholly resolved, by the promise of marriage between a tolerant Québécois and a bilingual English Quebecer. This time, however, the language of communication between the two is French. The intermarriage motif as a symbol of integration is also to be found in

Hugh Hood's *Game of Touch*, Gwethalyn Graham's *Earth and High Heaven*, Ron Sutherland's *Snow Lark*, and Elizabeth Spencer's short story, "Jean- Pierre," though in the two latter works, the potential for conflict continues even after the marriage.

The Montreal Jewish writers clearly share some of the preoccupations of their French and English colleagues. Like their French counterparts, they express a strong sense of cultural cohesiveness, but like their English colleagues they favour a tolerant, pluralistic environment in which Jews will be able to find a place. Some Jewish writers (e.g. A.M. Klein, Howard Roiter, Shulamis Yelin, and Abraham Boyarsky) carefully avoid any suggestions of assimilation into the larger community, while others (e.g. Richler, Abram Stilman, Herman Buller) present situations in which the relationships between a Jewish protagonist and a gentile companion is resolutely opposed by the families. On the other hand, the protagonists of these fictions are greatly attracted to the world beyond their own community. That world may take the form of status acquired through money (as with Duddy Kravitz), Marxist idealism (as with the young people in Ted Allan's *Love Is a Long Shot* and in Oscar Ryan's *Soon to Be Born*), *la vie en art* (as with the protagonists of Cohen's *The Favourite Game* and Richler's *Son of a Smaller Hero*), a more tolerant, liberal, unrestricted, cosmopolitan way of life (as favoured by practically all the Jewish writers), or the promise of a more sensuous, natural kind of love than appears possible in the conventional, middle-class, Jewish community (as we find in the short stories of Greta Nemiroff and Gerri Sinclair, and in the novels of Richler, Cohen, Ted Allan, Abraham Ram, and Donna Steinberg). I am referring here to the recurring delusion that far-away *shiksas* look *sheine*. The same phenomenon, incidentally, exists among Québécois writers, whose male protagonists are all too frequently lured by the charms of non-French females. In both cases, the women appear to be symbols of another mode of life, an escape from the conventions and restrictions of the bourgeois world.

In short, the Jewish protagonists of these fictions are characteristically tempted to integrate into the North American mainstream of secularism, moral relativism, sensuousness, and individual self-fulfilment—usually symbolized by the morally ambivalent *shiksa*, who is very often French. Thus Duddy Kravitz is attracted by Yvette; Eric Levy, the protagonist of Abram Stilman's novel, by Mariette; David Webber, the hero of Ted Allan's *Love Is a Long Shot*, by Marie; Morrie Cohen, the hero of Herman Buller's *One Man Alone*, by Philomine; and Arthur Meller, the hero of *Soon To Be Born,* by Gabrielle Lajeunesse; the other alluring gentiles are English (e.g. in two of Jerry Wexler's stories). It is no coincidence that some of these figures—Yvette, Gabrielle, and Philomine, for example—are associated with nature. The writer presumably wishes to suggest that gentile women are freer and more natural (faraway *shiksas* are greener)! To a greater or lesser extent, the Jewish protagonist is rebelling against the collective values of family, clan, community, more often than not symbolized by the protagonist's mother as in the work of Richler, Leonard Cohen, Abraham Ram, Gerri Sinclair, Donna Steinberg, or occasionally by a grandfather, as in Richler's *Son of a Smaller Hero* and *The Apprenticeship of Duddy Kravitz*.

It is quite rare in Jewish Montreal literature, however, to find a protagonist who succeeds in establishing a permanent, satisfactory relationship with a gentile. The most unequivocal exception occurs in Oscar Ryan's *Soon to be Born*. In that novel, the Jewish hero, Arthur Meller, is happily married to Gabrielle Lajeunesse, a francophone woman of rural origin. This time the opposition does not come from the families, for Ryan in concerned with the class struggle, not with the politics of integration. In two of Richler's novels—*St. Urbain's Horseman* and *Joshua Then and Now*—the hero is married to a gentile, but their relationship is troubled at times by protests from the family of one of the partners—his mother in the first novel, her father in the second.

In most cases, the Jewish protagonist pulls out of the relationship, or the gentile breaks it off, or the opposition from the parents makes it impossible even to begin. I call this recurring conflict that pits loyalty to family, community, and culture against North American secularism "ambiguous integration," because though the Jewish protagonists long for and often choose the freedom of the wider world around them, it cannot be achieved without sacrificing much of what is precious in their heritage. In the end, the protagonist frequently remains alone, and his/her ultimate fate is left unresolved or unstated.

I would like briefly to show how this conflict is worked out in several of the novels. Let us consider, first of all, what is involved when the Jewish partner breaks off the relationship. In Richler's *Son of a Smaller Hero*, Noah Adler drops Miriam Hall, and in Cohen's *The Favourite Game*, Breavman drops Shell. In both cases the hero prefers to be true to the call of his future vocation rather than luxuriate in love, sex, and the inevitable entanglements of domesticity. In Donna Steinberg's *I Lost It All in Montreal* the heroine, Shayna Pearl, ultimately separates from a biker-rock musician, who is nominally Jewish, but whose name, Peter Freeman, implies that he represents the freedom and moral relativism of gentile North America. In similar fashion, she prefers to establish her own identity and career rather than serve the needs of a man who would turn her into his housekeeper.

In some novels, the gentile initiates the rupture in the relationship. Thus in Abram Stilman's *Mariette*, it is the Québécoise heroine who decides she can neither give up her Catholicism nor expect her Jewish lover (Eric Levy) to give up his religion for her. So Mariette calls off the engagement. Interestingly in *Levy,* the other Stilman novel I read, the hero's Westmount girlfriend, Virginia Porter, follows her lover to Israel. Presumably they will live happily ever after on his kibbutz. Levy, though crippled in the war, makes no concessions in love. It is Virginia who will have to give up her identity and integrate herself into Jewish life in Israel. For Abram Stilman there can be no assimilation of Jews into Canadian life. In Richler's *Apprenticeship* it is Yvette who breaks with Duddy, not for religious or cultural reasons, but because he is morally bankrupt.

In some of the earlier fictions, parental disapproval is sufficiently powerful to disrupt relationships between Jews and gentiles before they can develop into marriages. For Abram Stilman, the principal obstacle to intermarriage lies in the attitudes of the families concerned. On the gentile side, it is good old-fashioned anti-Semitism; on the Jewish side, at least in the novel *Mariette*, the parents of Eric Levy are overly devoted to the Levy family tradition. Thus Eric and Mariette are, like Romeo and Juliet, star-crossed lovers from opposing families. In the two Richler novels where an intermarriage has already taken place—*St. Urbain's Horseman* and *Joshua Then and Now*—the families at first reject but later accept the marriage. The couple emerge from the vicissitudes of the plot stronger than ever in their love for each other. Though both Hersh and Joshua have a strong sense of Jewish identity, they have no religious affiliation to Judaism. Conveniently, their wives too are indifferent to religion. So for Richler there is no real obstacle to integration.

We will turn now to the work of somewhat younger writers. In Gerri Sinclair's story, "The Hoist," the child's father informs his little girl that she won't ever be able to marry Sadja, the genial Yugoslav steelworker, because he isn't Jewish. In Greta Nemiroff's "Seder," the impact of the family culture is so strong that the teenage protagonist, Helen Markheimer, will never be tempted to return to the West Indian world she has encountered for the first time. In both stories, however, the issue is as much a question of class as it is a question of Jewish identity. It would seem that in fiction at least allegiance to an ethnic or religious affiliation is slipping.

Having established the pervasiveness of the desire to merge into the wider gentile community, I would like to consider just what it is that the Jewish protagonists fear to lose if they take the plunge. The major concern is the loss of family ties, for it is somehow taken for granted that the Jewish parents will not be able to accept the mixed marriage of their errant son or daughter, that the Jew who marries a gentile is adopting a way of life that cannot include the Jewish parents. Granted the strictness of orthodox Jewish dietary laws and the way that Jewish family life often revolves around the festivals, it is easy to see the basis for the assumption. Ironically, however, most of the families described in Montreal Jewish fiction are not so orthodox as to make compromise impossible. Norman Levine, Oscar Ryan, Jerry Wexler, and Richler describe mixed marriages, but only in *Joshua Then and Now* is there any integration of families. Richler presents it comically, but it could be given serious treatment.

An extreme statement of parental disapproval occurs in a story by Norman Levine, plaintively titled "Why Do You Live So Far Away?" In it, the Jewish narrator admits to his sister that at the time of his marriage to his gentile wife he had pretended to his family that she was half

Jewish: "I said that long ago because of Maw... She said if this [had] happened in her time the family would be sitting *shiva* (*She'll Only Drag You Down* 77). That is to say, the parents would have disowned their son and regarded him as dead. Almost as extreme is the attitude of Noah's grandfather in Richler's *Son of a Smaller Hero*: "Go, become a Goy... Go join, become my enemy" (203). It is clear that if he goes abroad, Noah will be accused of abandoning his family and his community, and this is what Noah finds most difficult about his leave taking. In Cohen's *The Favourite Game*, Breavman is aware of the guilt trip laid on him by his mother, yet he too persists in his course of action. Even Shayna Pearl, the heroine of *I Lost It All in Montreal*, recognizes that the greatest obstacle to a freer life in the secular world is her mother:

> Oh, Christ, what am I saying? I don't want her to die! She's my mother and I love her. I care what she thinks of me... Life would be so much easier if I just despised her. Then I wouldn't have to worry about disappointing her when I tell her that my future plans include, among other things, being a career woman and moving into my own place in downtown Montreal—or maybe even Los Angeles. And she will be disappointed... she's laid down the law as far as I'm concerned; no daughter of Sylvia and Arnie Fine M.D., (Ob. Gyn) leaves home without making a pit stop at the local synagogue to exchange vows.
>
> (*I Lost It All in Montreal* 8-9)

A second but less important reason why Jewish protagonists hesitate to merge into the gentile world has to do with their reluctance to abandon a culture or way of life. We get a rare glimpse into the aesthetic pleasures of synagogue worship in Cohen's *Favourite Game*:

> When he saw the rabbi and cantor move in their white robes, the light on the brocaded letters of their prayer shawl; when he stood among his uncles and bowed with them and joined his voice to theirs in the responses; when he followed in the prayer book the catalogue of magnificence—
>
> (*The Favourite Game* 104)

Breavman is attracted to the ritual, but he expresses his disappointment that the worshippers have lost their fervour:

> No, his uncles were not grave enough. They were strict, not grave. They did not seem to realize how fragile the ceremony was. They participated in it blindly, as if it would last forever. They did not seem to realize how important they were, not self-important, but important to the incantation, the altar, the ritual. They were ignorant of the craft of devotion. They were merely devoted. They never thought how close the ceremony was to chaos. Their nobility was insecure because it rested on inheritance and not moment-to-moment creation in the face of annihilation.
>
> (*The Favourite Game* 104)

Apart from A.M. Klein, Leonard Cohen is the only Montreal Jewish writer who expresses some pleasure in Jewish religious observance.

If Jewish protagonists retain their ties to the Jewish community it is because of familial and cultural loyalties. In Jerry Wexler's short story, "The Bequest," the Jewish protagonist separates from his gentile wife and returns to the St. Urbain Street district where he grew up. He explains his actions in terms of a vague search for roots:

> Perhaps it was my East European heritage that made me more volatile. I used to say that my collective unconscious lay on the steppes of the Ukraine, in villages where the huts had mud floors and women screamed at their children and husbands, while her [his gentile wife's] collective unconscious lay in a tea room in the Isle of Wight.
>
> (*The Bequest* 18)

Helen Markheimer, the adolescent protagonist of Greta Nemiroff's two Montreal stories, though embarrassed by her parents' Austrian emigré behaviour, has nonetheless adopted their taste for high culture. She longs to break out of the protective net of luxury that they have woven about her, but finds in the end that she prefers the apparent solidity of their values over the tawdry and sordid reality she discovers in south end Montreal. Familial and cultural ties are strong in Montreal Jewish fiction. Consequently Jewish protagonists who wish to cut loose from their moorings will have to be prepared to sail some stormy seas. Though Oscar Ryan, Norman Levine, and Richler permit satisfactory cross-cultural marriages in their work, the protagonists have to cope with family harassment and their own feelings of guilt.

We can detect three states of mind in Montreal Jewish fiction, but they are not chronological. It is not that the older writers see no possibility for integration, and that the younger ones do. It is much more a question of the writer's familiarity with Jewish culture and traditional values. The work of such writers as A.M. Klein, Shulamis Yelin, Abram Stilman, Jack Ludwig, Hilda Shubert, Abraham Boyarsky, and Howard Roiter reveals a closeness to Jewish culture—either because the writers were themselves immigrants or because they remained attached to the traditional religious culture of their upbringing. Consequently, they integrate Jewish culture in their work to the point that they may appear to be aiming mainly at a Jewish audience. Needless to say, for these writers there is no integration into the gentile community.

The second group includes Oscar Ryan, Irving Layton, Ted Allan, Jerry Wexler, Abraham Ram, Norman Levine, Mordecai Richler, Leonard Cohen, C.J. Newman, and Gerri Sinclair. Although their work lacks the same closeness to Jewish experience that the work of the first group has, it may nonetheless express extreme anguish and guilt in breaking away from family ties. It is clear that this group is aiming at an audience far beyond the Jewish community. Some of these writers received an adequate Jewish education in their childhood years, but we don't feel in them the same attempt to build a bridge between *yiddishkayt* (roughly Jewish culture) and the English language that we do in the work of say A.M. Klein or even Jack Ludwig. On the contrary, we easily detect in people like Irving Layton, Ted Allan, Abraham Ram, Norman Levine, Robyn Sarah, and Richler, the sense of pain and loss that comes from rejecting a tradition imbibed in childhood years. These writers are very much concerned with the relation between the Jew and the gentile community.

The work of a third group of writers consisting of Greta Nemiroff, Seymour Blicker, Oscar Ryan, and Donna Steinberg, is further removed from cultural or religious affiliation. The protagonists in their novels and stories express very little pain over abandonment of Jewish cultural identity, because they do not appear to have ever been deeply immersed in it. Although these fictions deal with Jewish characters and sometimes provide a liberal sprinkling of Yiddishisms, they provide only a superficial treatment of Jewish values or culture. I am not suggesting that their work lacks merit, but merely that it contains nothing profoundly Jewish, and this I venture to predict may be the wave of the future.

To conclude, we cannot help noticing that there has been a falling off in Jewish content and consciousness in the Montreal Jewish novel. Though most of the major writers mentioned here are still producing, there do not appear to be any obvious replacements for A.M. Klein, Irving Layton, Mordecai Richler, Leonard Cohen, Jack Ludwig, or C.J. Newman. The only person still writing from within the Jewish tradition is the novelist Abraham Boyarsky. The others write about Jews, rather than Jewish issues, from a somewhat distant perspective. No major force has emerged from among the younger group of Montreal Jews writing in English. So in one sense Eli Mandel is quite correct: there has been a gradual decline in Canadian Jewish writing—at least insofar as its Jewishness is concerned. This may have something to do with the disappearance of the ghetto, the openness of Canadian society, and the attractiveness of North American culture.

There is, however, a new element to be considered: the French Jewish community is now firmly established in Montreal. It has already produced such notable writers as Monique Bosco, Naïm Kattan, and Régine Robin, and we may expect others to emerge in future. But as far as the English-Jewish writers are concerned, it seems likely that in the absence of a Jewish consciousness to interpret, explain, and defend, their work will gradually become indistinguishable from the concerns of other Montrealers writing in English. The so-called three solitudes will return to two, and the pull towards integration may become less ambiguous.

Allan, Ted (1916-1995)
"My Zaida" 1949, *Lies My Father Told Me* 1975, *Love Is a Long Shot* 1984, *Don't You Know Anybody Else* 1985

Blicker, Seymour (1940-
Shmucks 1972, *The Last Collection* 1976

Boyarsky, Abraham (1946-
A Pyramid of Time 1978, *Shreiber* 1981

Buller, Herman (1927-
One Man Alone 1963

Cohen, Leonard (1934-
The Favourite Game 1963, *Beautiful Losers* 1966, *Death of a Lady's Man* 1977

Hofmann Nemiroff, Greta (1937-
"Chez Sergei" 1981, "Seder" 1985

Klein, A.M. (1909-72)
The Second Scroll 1951, *Short Stories* 1983

Layton, Irving (1912-
Six stories from *The Swinging Flesh* 1961

Levine, Norman (1923-
"In Montreal" 1958, *From A Seaside Town* ("She'll Only Drag You Down") Chaps. 6, 8, 12-14, 1970, "The English Girl" 1971

Ludwig, Jack (1922-
A Woman of Her Age 1973

Newman, C.J. (1935-
We Always Take Care of Our Own 1965, "Yenteh" 1969

Ram, Abraham (1919?-
The Noise of Singing 1976, Dark of Caves 1977, Once in Woods 1982

Richler, Mordecai (1931-
Son of a Smaller Hero 1955, *The Apprenticeship od Duddy Kravitz* 1959, *The Street* 1969, *St. Urbain's Horseman* 1971, *Joshua Then and Now* 1980, *Solomon Gursky* 1989, *Oh Canada! Oh Quebec!* 1992

Roiter, Howard (1939-
Here Comes Hymie! 1990

Ryan, Oscar (1904-
Soon to Be Born 1980

Sarah, Robyn (1949-
"New Management" 1988, "A Minor Incident"

Shubert, Hilda (1936-
They Came From Kernitza 1969
Sinclair, Gerri (1947-
"The Hoist" 1982
Steinberg, Donna (1954-
I Lost It All in Montreal 1983
Stilman, Abram (1903-
Mariette 1961, *Levy* 1971, Short Stories 1976
Weintraub, William (1926-
Why Rock the Boat? 1961, *The Underdogs* 1979
Wexler, Jerry (1950-
The Bequest 1984, "For Ann" 1984
Yelin, Shulamis (1913-
Shulamis: Stories From a Montreal Childhood 1983

CRITICAL READINGS IN MONTREAL JEWISH LITERATURE

Ages, Arnold. "Canadian Jewish Writing." *Chronicle Review*, Dec. 1972: 15-19.

Anctil, Pierre. "Les écrivains juifs de Montréal." *Juifs et réalités juives au Québec*. Ed. Pierre Anctil and Gary Caldwell. Quebec: IQRC, 1984: 195-252.

Arnold, Janice. "David Rome on Canadian Jewish Literature." *Chronicle Review,* Nov. 1975: 19, 21.

Butovsky, Mervin, et al. "Thoughts on Our Culture." *Viewpoints* 11.1, (Summer 1980): 22-27.

———. Afterword to Y. Zipper's *The Far Side of the River*. Oakville: Mosaic, 1985.

Edel, Leon. "Marginal Keri and Textual Chetiv." *The A.M. Klein Symposium*. Ed. Seymour Mayne. Ottawa: University of Ottawa Press, 1975.

Gerson, Carole. "Some Patterns of Exile in Jewish Writing of the Commonwealth." *Ariel* 13.4 (1982): 103-14.

Godard (Thompson), Barbara. "The City of Montreal in the English and French Canadian Novel 1945-65." M.A. Diss. Université de Montréal, 1967.

———. "The Geography of Separatism." *Laurentian University Review* 9.1 (Nov. 1976): 33-50.

Greenstein, Michael. "Beyond the Ghetto and the Garrison: Jewish Canadian Boundaries." *Mosaic* 14.2 (Spring 1981): 121-30.

———. *Third Solitudes: Tradition and Discontinuity in Jewish-Canadian Literature.* Montreal: McGill-Queen's, 1989.

Journal of Canadian Studies 19.2 (Summer 1984) A.M. Klein's Montreal.

Kattan, Naïm. "Le visage de Montréal vu par des romanciers de langue anglaise." *Présence de la critique: Critique et littérature contemporaines au Canada français.* Ed. Gilles Marcotte. Montreal: HMH, 1966: 187-94.

———. "Montreal and French-Canadian Culture. What They Mean to English Canadian Novelists." *Tamarack Review* 40 (Summer 1966): 40-53.

———. "Deux romanciers canadiens-anglais et Montréal." *Culture populaire et littératures au Québec.* Ed. René Bouchard. Saratoga: Anma Libri. Vol. 19 (1980): 257-63.

Lappin, Ben. "The Receding World of Abraham Klein." *Viewpoints* 2.4 (Spring 1981): 16-29.

Mandel, Eli. "The Fabled City: Themes of Exile and Return in Canadian-Jewish Writing." lecture 10 Dec. 1976.

———. "Ethnic Voices in Canadian Literature." in *Another Time.* Erin: Porcépic, 1977: 91-102.

Melançon, Benoît. "La Littérature montréalaise des communautés culturelles: prolégomènes et bibliographie." Montreal: Montréal imaginaire, Les Presses de l'Université de Montréal, 1990.

Nadel, Ira. *Jewish Writers of North America.* Detroit: Gale, 1981.

———. "The Absent Prophet in Canadian Jewish Fiction." *English Quarterly* 5 (Spring-Summer 1972): 83-92.

Nepveu, Pierre. "Les Juifs à Montréal: le tiers inclus?" *Montréal, L'invention juive.* Montreal: Montréal imaginaire, Les Presses de l'Université de Montréal, 1991. 73-86.

Robinson, Ira, P. Anctil & M. Butovsky, eds. *An Everyday Miracle: Yiddish Culture in Montreal.* Montreal: Véhicule, 1990.

Rome, David. "Literature of Jewish Canadians." *Jewish Book Annual* 18 (1960-61): 44-53.

———. "Jews in Canadian Literature, a Bibliography." 2 vols. Montreal: CJC & JPL, 1962.

———. *Recent Canadian Jewish Authors* and *La Langue française*. Montreal: Jewish Public Library, 1970.
———. "The Canadian Poets and the Immigrants." *JIAS News* 20.1 (March 1973): 3.
Rome, David, Judith Nefsky, & Paule Obermeier. *Les Juifs du Québec, bibliographie rétrospective annotée*. Quebec: IQRC, 1981. 190-217.
Simon, Sherry. "The Language of Difference. Minority Writers in Quebec." *Canadian Literature* Supp. No. 1 (May 1987): 119-28.
———. "Entre les langues: l'écriture juive contemporaine à Montréal." *Montréal, l'invention juive*. Montreal: Montréal imaginaire, Les Presses de l'Université de Montréal, 1991.87-102.
Sirois, Antoine. *Montréal dans le roman canadien*. Montreal Didier, 1968.
———. "Conquête horizontale et verticale de la ville." *Canadian Literature* 72 (Spring 1977): 45-8.
Stratford, Philip. "Romanciers et nouvellistes anglophones du Québec: 1970-80." *Protée* 10.2 (Summer 1982): 11-14.
Waddington, Miriam. Introduction to *Canadian Jewish Short Stories*. Ed. Miriam Waddington. Toronto: Oxford University Press, 1990.
Wolfe, Morris & Gerri Sinclair. Introduction. *The Spice Box: An Anthology of Jewish Canadian Writing*. Toronto: Lester & Orpen Dennys, 1981.

Irving Layton
The Invention of the Self

MERVIN BUTOVSKY

FOR NEARLY HALF A CENTURY, Irving Layton (b. 1912) has been a commanding presence on the Canadian literary scene. In a writing life that has seen the publication of over forty-five volumes—nearly a volume a year since his first offering in 1945—he has achieved celebrity status within Canada's cultural community as well as national recognition in the form of the country's premier literary prize, the Governor-General's Award, in 1959. He was named a Companion of the Order of Canada in 1976, a civic honor attesting to his position as a major contributor to his nation's literature.

While this reputation is based solidly on his poetry, Layton's voluminous output also comprises short fiction, essays, memoirs, reviews, correspondence, prefaces, and introductions, which, like his poems, all bear his unmistakeable signature. From his earliest poems, which appeared in small literary periodicals where Layton and his contemporaries sought to redirect Canada's staid, provincial culture toward the challenging modernist temper, Layton's work has always depended on a forceful, combative, representation of the self. Foregrounded in all his work is the perceiving mind—self-absorbed and self-observed—inviting the reader to share its perceptions only if accompanied by the often jarring presence of a seemingly undisguised narrator: the maker of the poem himself. The poem's reality is made available only on the condition that the reader accept the narrator's version of things. This pervasive egotism with its self-centered gestures has offended some; what they fail to recognize is that an esthetic as well as a temperamental urgency underlies its literary deployment. Layton confesses to his self-conscious performance when he describes the polarities of identity revealed in the poems: "I became by turns prophet and clown."

These self-selected personae are usually represented in the author's characteristic role as moral gadfly to his fellow Canadians, Jew and gentile alike, chastising their failings in a language of deliberate affront. Layton's open didacticism presupposes a privileged position for the poet in society. Everything that Layton has written expresses his conviction that the poet has a special role, signified by his preternatural power to see into the heart of things, and the capacity to make such revelations available to the unawakened reader. This romantic sense of vocation to which he clings (and which now separates him from most younger poets who no longer share its claims) has resulted in a self-created retrospective myth which encapsulates his deepest insights into himself and his transaction with the world.

What his vast number of poems collectively signify is that Layton is a mythographer whose central myth is concerned with the act of self-creation. His life-long act of writing has produced no single poem more impressive than his assertive, hectoring self, a mock-heroic figure who invented just the kind of person he had to become if he was to deliver himself from the obscurity and ineffectuality that had engulfed others around him. Layton brought to his chosen literary vocation much the same raw, dynamic energy that his peers from the first immigrant generation were to demonstrate when they elbowed their way out of urban slums into the often inhospitable fields of law, medicine, business, and manufacturing.

The mythic outline that emerges from Layton's account describes the crucial transformative acts that have resulted in his own being. At an early age he rejected the identity which birth and history had given him and for many years remained uncertain about his choice of an appropriate identity that would signify his fluid, evolving sense of self. His birth name was Yisroel Pinchas Lazarovitch, but this underwent considerable change—Issie Lazarovitch, Isadore Lazarre, Irvine Lazarre, Pete Lazarovitch, Irvine Layton, Irving Peter Layton—before he was to arrive at the one most suited to his emerging character and vocation. Whatever his motives, these changes indicate a desire to efface the foreign-sounding Yiddish-Slavic original and replace it with the more acceptable anglicized version announced in his final choice. Thus the numerous variations can be read as the most immediate tokens of ethnic discomfort; countless others of his generation similarly accepted name-changes as the least painful way of entering a society whose social practices often penalized ethnic particularity. In Layton's case, the indeterminacy of name also signals a restlessness with the state of ethnic fixity and a willingness to venture into new experience as a radical innocent, unencumbered by the past.

Layton was born in Romania and brought to Canada on his first birthday in 1913. The family lived in the crowded Jewish quarter south of Ontario Street which Layton described as "a semi-slum area inhabited by French-Canadians, Jews, and Italians who lived on de Montigny street, a very rich and very colourful neighbourhood comprising a number of cat-houses, small grocery stores, immigrants." The ethnic and social distinctions inscribed in his immediate neighbourhood gave him his first lesson in boundaries, oppositions, and limits. Remembering later what he had unconsciously absorbed from his environment, Layton described how Montreal's cityscape contributed to his own sense of otherness:

> In Montreal the dominant ethnic groups stared at one another balefully across their self-erected ghetto walls. Three solitudes. I remember the feelings of anxiety I had as a boy whenever I crossed St. Denis Street. This street marked the border between the Jewish and French-Canadian territories. East of St. Denis was hostile Indian country densely populated with church-going Mohawks somewhat older than myself waiting to ambush me... Bleury Street and beyond, walking westward, took me into that other ghetto, the one where the Anglo-Saxons lived in tree-lined and privileged aloofness... So that when I found myself in Westmount...I'd feel a different kind of menace. One that was internal rather than external in its thrust. I felt weak, helpless, as if all my strength was leaving me through the pores of my skin. Here I always felt myself to

> be a trespasser, not a warrior as I did when I crossed St. Denis Street. At any moment huge mastiffs would be loosed on me or someone with a healthy tanned face would say to me with cold but perfect English diction: "Get away from here."
>
> (Foreword, *Collected Poems*, 1971)

But the lesson of the streets was a generalized social version of what the young boy was already intimately acquainted with at home. In his own parents Layton had an immediate, indelible exposure to the existence of self-enclosed personalities who, in their distinctive individuality, represented to him the irreconcilable polar extremes of temperament and sensibility. In them he first experienced the clash of opposites what was to be transmuted into the typical dialectical mode of his mature thought.

Layton's father had been a bookkeeper in the old country, but he was unable to adjust to the new economic realities in Canada. A deeply religious man, his answer to the disappointments and frustrations of daily life was to retreat into a world of his own making, shutting out the clamorous surroundings by concentrating on the spiritual reality he found in holy writ. In the son's memory the father is more often aching absence than affirming presence. The closed door to the father's study-room, which provided the privacy and solitude for his spiritual contemplations, also shut out the actual world of striving, contest, and engagement. The father's withdrawal left the mother to cope with family's economy and welfare. She was an energetic, argumentative woman, who supported the family by maintaining a small grocery store in the converted living-room of their flat. Unlike the father, she was forceful, demanding, and vituperative—traits which Layton claims as her legacy to his idiosyncratic stance and bearing.

In the father's quiescence and the mother's assertiveness Layton had the basic polarities for his "family romance," his personal myth of origin. In parental conflict he located the primal antinomies that formed the basis of his character and from which he derived the dialectical structure of thought and feeling that is manifest in all his writing. The terms of the configuration may vary: feeling/form; carnal/spiritual; self/world; Jew/Christian or Idd/Xian; academic/poet; critic/writer; cock/cunt;

life/death; appetite/restraint; contemplation/immersion; communism/democracy; compassion/cruelty; ugliness/beauty;— but regardless of specific subject, it was in the antithetical coupling of opposites that he perceived the nature of reality, and the juxtaposition of contraries became his chief means for exploring its infinite variety.

This paradigm also informs Layton's attitude to his Jewish identity which is predicated on the distinction between Judaism and being Jewish, on a strict demarcation between the religious and the socio-cultural components of Jewish life. He early rejected the religious rituals and daily practices of Judaism as too narrow and irrelevant for modern usage. In his memoir *Waiting For The Messiah* (1985), he refers to the religious dimension of Judaism as a "legacy of my father's superstition and the foolish rigidities that went along with it." Elsewhere he softens this view by enlarging on the praiseworthy, contemplative devotion evinced by his father. But the emphatic dismissal of his father's ritual practices as mere "superstition" and "rigidities" is a candid account of his youthful attitude, recalling for us something of his desire to dispense with his father's archaisms in order that he might align himself with the new social and political forces then manifest throughout the immigrant community, offering the younger generation a radically altered discourse to replace the outmoded one still based on traditional religious practices.

This process of transference from one belief system to another was doubtless affected by the economic upheaval of the Great Depression and the specific political circumstances confronting Jews in Canada and, particularly, Quebec. During the 1930s the raw immigrant community, the majority of whom had barely landed in Canada in their flight from Czarist anti-Semitism, watched with mounting dismay and horror the entrapment of their European families. On the streets of Montreal, meanwhile, they nervously observed the rise of indigenous xenophobic, Catholic and fascist sentiment, openly demonstrated in public rallies and street parades. These manifestations centred on the Jews, demanding a restriction to their entry as refugees and a curtailment of their economic activities. To many, it seemed that the murderous conditions of Europe had now overtaken their haven in Canada.

Little wonder that the appeal of left-wing movements opposed to fascism and Naziism was so wide-spread among Jewish youth. Like many other self-respecting members of his generation, Layton gravitated to the socialist groups which, in their intense polemical discussions, internationalist orientation, and fierce debates with competing factions, served as a kind of finishing school while he attended Baron Byng High School and during his college years at MacDonald.

Both his formal education and the deep involvement in Marxist movements offered secular alternatives to the disparaged Judaism of his father. The grammar of political science acquired at university (he took an MA degree in the subject following his B.Sc. at MacDonald) and the universalistic ethic of socialism became the surrogates for the antiquated vocabulary of tradition. Layton, whose education in the literature and religious thought of Judaism never went beyond the elementary *cheder* level, found in the secular version of history and human destiny an intellectual seriousness that was absent from his experience with Judaism. And the clash between these particularistic and universalistic world views had a profound influence on the representation of Jewish experience in his poetry.

Thus a reading of the Layton's work reveals two distinct stages in the evolution of his attitude to the literary treatment of Jewish circumstance. In the first stage, which comprises the poetry from the 1940s to the mid-60s, he is only intermittently concerned with the circumstances of Jewish life, and rarely are the poems concerned with the narrator's awareness of himself as Jew. When he does draw upon Jewish character or incident the poems are often blunt indictments against bloated materialism or moral indifference. His targets are usually middle-class suburbanites, indifferent both to Torah and poetry. So in "The Real Values" the narrator commiserates with the hapless rabbi of such a congregation, asking:

> Rabbi, why do you move heaven and earth
> to blow breath
> into this lifeless body,
> drowned under the surfeit

of Chinese food and pizzapie?

and concludes by admonishing him to

Save your breath, rabbi.
No, save your money.

And learn from your bloated flock
bored by whiskey and wifeswapping,
the burnt offerings on Sunday,
how to invest sensibly
in real estate values.

So that you can speak the truth
as I do.

The inversion of values which sees the congregation's materialism subvert the rabbi's vain attempt to quicken their spirits, is expended in the punning "real estate values." Here is a fair example of Layton's moralistic verse focussed on the Jewish community or its representatives. The didactic intent is revealed in the plain, prosaic language. It eschews any form of figuration, relying instead on the speaking voice of a narrator who has access to a truth obviously withheld from the well-intentioned but deluded rabbi.

The attitude toward middle-class Jews reflected in this poem is typical of the many caustic lines Layton directed to his own people. In poems such as "The Ritual Cut," "The Human Condition," and "Stocktaking on the Day of Atonement," one has the reiterated disdain at the moral failings he finds in the community, failings he identifies with middle-class affluence and complacency. Writing in the "Foreward" to *Europe and Other Bad News* (1981) he states that this attitude formed when he had "experienced the banalities of middle-class Judaism and gotten to know from first-hand experience its bottomless contempt for anything that doesn't contribute to personal advancement measured in terms of money and chattels. It was a spectacle to make a poet weep or explode with rage. I have done both."

But just as all of Layton's poetry can be divided between the declarative and the contemplative, so too his poetry on Jewish themes. If his social commentary on the modern Jewish condition speaks with one voice, there is at the same time another type of expression which invokes his Jewish experience in a different register. In such poems the narrator does not castigate at the sight of imperfection, but draws upon the memory of his origins as a means of self-exploration. The speaking voice turns in on itself, seeking in the remembered past some touchstone to its own true nature. The self-reflective act of memory leads to insights which, ironically, go beyond egotism and self-aggrandizement. For example, "Gothic Landscape" (1951) presents a winter scene as reconstructed in "my Jewboy mind." The narrator's use of the insulting term to identify himself makes explicit the anxiety he is compelled to feel as an outsider. The poem opens with his description of wintry trees:

> They stand like penitential Augustines
> These trees; and in my Jewboy mind they are monks.
> Brown-robed, fearful after their long sleep in dungeons;

and then proceeds to explain that the imagistic transference of trees to monks lies in their fearful austerity and an imagined childhood escapade:

> When I was a child one of them nearly caught me,
> But I escaped, tunnelling the snow to my mother's face;
> Under her grey shawl I saw God's Assyrian beard,
> And a page of *lameds* racing toward me like ostriches.

Wintry cold and dormant nature may be likened to monastic orders, but comfort is to be found in a mother's face and her proximity to the divine, pictured in the familiar schoolboy image of an ancient bearded warrior, whose chargers are transformed to the picturesque Hebrew letter shaped like an ostrich. The second stanza goes beyond the imagistic comparison between winter's blight and monastic severity by introducing the mature narrator's awareness of the Jewish persecutions suffered at the hands of monks during the Spanish Inquisition—thus revealing the historical source of his fear and dread:

> I've taken no vow not to forget
> The torquemadas stirring in the frosty veins:
> But the cloister bells deafen me with insults,
> And the sallowfaced acolytes inform
> The snowdrifts what to whisper against me;
> Autos-de fe make red the immaculate sky;

The use of the present tense tells us that the imprint of history still informs his reading of nature and man; he is pledged to remembrance. The concluding lines call for the return of the revifying sun which would restore the lost vitality—a fecund nature and a passionate Christ:

> Come soon, O bright Tudor sun!
> I do not like this monastic whiteness of winter—
> It is a Christ drained of all blood.

The life-denying frozen landscape is imaged as the bloodless body: winter is nature's blight symmetrical with the monk's despolation of Christ. This central juxtaposition is embedded in Jewish memory which reads the signification of the ice-bound landscape as the work of fearful, Christian zealots.

Taken together, Layton's poems based on a Jewish subject matter, whether written in a spirit of social criticism or introspection, are less frequent in the first twenty years of his publishing history than his other topical or philosophic concerns. The same can be noted in his critical or social commentary. In a period which comprised the two major events in modern Jewish history—the Holocaust and the establishment of a sovereign Jewish state—Layton's voice is only seldom heard, his attention was elsewhere, devoted to the subjects which preoccupied him in the first stage of his career: the dialectical nature of reality; the definition of an indigenous Canadian literary identity in the post-colonial world; the open recognition of our sexual natures.

In this respect, Layton is far more typical of the shared attitude of his time than his obstreperous individuality might suggest. From its beginnings in urban poverty, his life describes the familiar route of the modern Jewish intellectual's odyssey. It traces the young immigrant's awakening to secular ideas through education; the rupture from traditional belief; the espousal of radical political ideologies in the 1930s and 1940s; the formulation of a cosmopolitan humanistic credo beyond the boundaries of religious or ethnic particularities. These mark the stages of Layton's development just as they describe the path taken by numerous other sons and daughters of immigrants on their way to fuller participation in the host culture. And Layton's poetry written between the end of World War II and 1967 exemplifies this tendency toward the universalization of culture and values. Throughout this period his poetic reflections on Jewish experience were mainly refracted through his general philosophic and political concerns.

But since 1967 a significant change can be noted in his relationship to Jews and Judaism, signalling an open identification with Jewish national circumstance: politically, in support of beleaguered Israel, and morally, in his condemnation of Christianity as the fomentor of the anti-Semitism which culminated in the Holocaust. In his characteristically resolute fashion, Layton reacted dramatically to Israel's threatened position in the days leading up to the Six-Day War. Struck by the indifference of the great powers before the loudly-trumpeted invasion plans by Israel's surrounding enemies, he saw the imminent destruction of the Jewish state as a continuation of the genocidal sentiments of Christian Europe. Little wonder then that with the unexpected victory came an outpouring of pride in the Israeli military power which had assured the State's existence against overwhelming odds. In fact Layton perceived the military victory of the modern Israeli as a kind of redress for the powerlessness of the historic Jew. In his "For My Two Sons, Max and David" he juxtaposes a lengthy catalogue description of Jewish victimization, beginning with:

> The wandering Jew: the suffering Jew
> The despoiled Jew: the beaten Jew
> The Jew to burn: the Jew to gas
> The Jew to humiliate

and continues with a list of prosaic sentences each beginning emphatically with "The Jew..." and then specifying a trait whereby the Jew's scapegoat role justified Christian depredations. These include:

The Jew whose helplessness stirs the heart and conscience
  of the Christian like the beggars outside his churches

The Jew who can justifiably be murdered because he is rich
  The Jew who can justifiably be murdered because he is poor
...
The Jew no one can live with: he has seen too many conquerors
  come and vanish, the destruction of too many empires

Against this account of the Jews' historic moral mission and its consequences, which he appears to be recalling as an instructive lesson for his children, the final three lines of the poem charges them to alter their Jewish fate by replacing powerlessness with power:

Be none of these my sons
My sons be none of these
Be gunners in the Israeli Air Force

The very bluntness of the final assertion makes its own claim for a reversal of the traditional role of the Jew which had exposed a defenceless people to continual persecution. In a world chagrined by the Jew's spiritual endowments which often inspired its enemies' murderous rages, it is prudent to rely on force, and break, once and for all, the mold of pariah/scapegoat, exchanging cringing weakness for virile sovereignty.

In a similar vein, "The New Sensibility" speaks to the need of poets to adapt to the new twentieth century condition of violence and moral hypocrisy. Formerly, the poets

who dish out the familiar idealistic crap
always make the murderous crowd
slobber

preparatory to prodding them with the sticks
and pouring gasoline on their cadavers

Now, however, the poet must no longer lend himself to such artful sentimentality. Instead

The up-to-date poet
besides labouring at his craft
should be a dead shot

Do you hear me Old Man?
a dead shot
sending the bullet
winging like a finished stanza
straight between the eyes

That's the new poetry
minted June 1967
in Tel Aviv and Sinai

I thought
I should let you know

If the sight of an Israel willing to take upon itself the full responsibility for its own survival (what the theologian Emil Fackenheim calls the Jewish return to history) induces in Layton a sense of national pride, and gives rise to these and other such poems which celebrate strength, heroism, and independence, they have been overshadowed by the chief ideological burden of the poems since the late 1960s: Christianity's guilt for the destruction of the European Jews. In countless poems, buttressed by tough-minded introductory statements to his recent collections, he assumes the stance of prosecutor demanding admission and confession from the Christian world for its culpability in furnishing the theological rationale which, in the course of European history, dehumanized the Jews and ultimately led to the death camps. To his long-standing view of Christianity as oppressor of human sexuality and natural vitality, he now added the direct responsibility for the Holocaust:

> It was Christianity that carefully prepared and seeded the ground on which Europe's gas chambers and crematoria flourished. The beginnings of antisemitism are rooted in the mendacious New Testament, where the lie of deicide is forged and foisted on the inhabitants of Judea and succeeding generations of Jews. It was at the Council of Nicea that Jews were officially labelled the murderers of Lord Jesus, and Christians were severely warned against having any commerce with them. It was a pope who invented the Roman ghetto; it was not Hitler but another pope who with Christian charity and tenderness dreamed up the distinguishing yellow Badge of Shame.
>
> The anti-sexuality, anti-life bias at the heart of Christianity contained in its terrible unfolding logic the extermination of six million human beings.
>
> ("Foreword," *For My Brother Jesus*, 1976)

Translated to poetry, Layton's accusatory charges are sometimes—as in "For Jesus Christ"—nearly reiterated prose statements:

> One pontiff invented the ghetto;
> more tender and loving, another commanded
> shivering ghosts to wear out its cobblestones
> warmed by the yellow Star of David.

until the final stanza where the innocent Jesus is told of the crimes committed in his name in a piercing image which links the related Christian and Nazi symbols, both inescapably implicated as instruments of torture:

> Your stoutest, most selfless partisans in Europe
> laboured nearly two thousand years
> to twist your Cross into the Swastika
> that tore into our flesh like a fish-hook.

In mounting his critique against Christianity, Layton has scrupulously differentiated the historical Jesus from the Church that arose in his name, claiming the former as fellow-Jew and Prophet, while attributing a perverse pathological degeneracy to the latter. To avoid any ambiguity and, one gathers, to prevent Christians from seeking comfort in the exemplary humane deeds of their founder, he has introduced the term Xians and Xianity to denote the barbaric condition of the Church and its adherents. The poem "Xianity" addresses Jesus as "Brother and fellow-poet" and proceeds to ask "is this what you wanted?" The answer to that rhetorical question sums up Layton's assessment of decayed Xianity:

> The mutterings of bead-counting hysterics?
> The snuffling of joyless misfits and cripples
> fearful of death, more fearful of life?
> the *misereres* of the doomed dregs
> in every large metropolis in the world?
> The hosannahs of the conformist hordes
> stinking of money and respectability?

The idea that the teachings of the Jewish Jesus have been misread by the Xians, and that the rightful heirs to his spiritual grace are the Jews, derives more from Layton's persistent dionysian conception of creativity through joy than from any consistent religious notions. Certainly, the appropriation of Jesus by the Jews has seldom been a popular issue amongst Jews, nor has it been often espoused in Rabbinic or modern Judaic literature. Hence, one suspects that Layton's insistence on reclaiming Jesus as brother and fellow-poet owes more to his need for the independent rebellious gesture—against Xianity and traditional Judaism both—than to articulating a post-holocaust theology based on the sundering of the historical Jesus from the deeds done in his name.

For the poetic act of reclaiming Jesus—the most often-addressed subject of his poetry in recent years—does more than merely add one more figure to the pantheon which includes the writers and thinkers with whom Layton identifies; it also illumines his conception of Jewish tradition and the true nature of the Jew. Detached from any abiding religious authority, he has assembled a personal genealogy, secular in orientation and eclectic in scope. It accommodates the Hebrew Prophets and Freud, Spinoza, Heine, and Marx, Jesus and Israeli soldiers, Babel and Mandelstam. A gathering of such figures suggests that their attractiveness lies less with their intrinsic Judaism than with some peculiar trait that Layton chooses to identify as Jewish. From these and other sources he has distilled what he considers their essential spiritual Jewish qualities: unyielding moral purpose, and a heroic assertion of will in the face of human waste and decay. Jewish history is a text whose narrative returns time and again to these themes, pronouncing on the fate of the prophetic seers who articulate divine will in order to reform social conduct and value, those whose exemplary behaviour proves a constant rebuke to the ways of the majority. But, as Layton sees it, such an account also describes the life of the poet. Being a minority people dedicated to a divine calling is to define oneself constantly against the uncomprehending majority; similarly, being a poet is to contend with the difference between visionary insight and the routine reality of the dull-eyed public. In this parallelism between Jewish history and artistic vocation, Layton has found a way of returning to an attachment he had been indifferent to in his youth. His selective reconstruction of a usable Jewish past—judging from the post-1960s poems—has been a potent source of energy from which the inventor of many selves finally takes on the guise he had revoked at the beginning of his illustrious career: the self-proclaiming, identifiable Jew, eternally troubled and troubling.

Works Cited

Layton, Irving. *Collected Poems*. Toronto: McClelland & Stewart, 1971.
_____. *For My Brother Jesus*. Toronto: McClelland & Stewart, 1976.
_____. *Europe and Other Bad News*. Toronto: McClelland & Stewart, 1981.
_____. *Waiting for the Messiah*. Toronto: McClelland & Stewart, 1985.

Glossary

ASHKENAZI	Jew of Central or Eastern European origins.
BIMA	Platform in synagogue where the Torah scroll is read
BOCHERIM	Young men, especially with reference to Yeshiva students
CEGEP	Colleges which are part of the Quebec educational system bridging the gap between Secondary and University studies.
CHACHMAH	lit. "wise woman"
CHEDER	Traditional name for Hebrew elementary school.
CHUTZPA	Effrontry, "cheek."
DHIMMA	Member of minority religious community within an Islamic country.
FARRETER	Traitor
GOY	Non-Jew.
HALAKHAH	System of rabbinic law.
HASIDIM	Groups of Orthodox Jews who are led by charismatic rabbinic leaders.
HAVDALAH	Judaic ceremony separating between Sabbaths/ holidays and weekdays.
KASHRUT	Judaic dietary laws.
KIDDUSH	Judaic ceremony inaugurating Sabbath and festival meals.
KOSHER	Something deemed proper according to the Judaic dietary laws.
KULTURKAMPF	Struggle between opposing ideologies.
MACHREK	Middle Eastern Countries.
MAGHREB	North Africa, Morocco.
MECHITZAH	Partition separating mens' and womens' sections of an Orthodox synagogue.
MIDRASH	Rabbinic legends.
MIMOUNA	Festival celebrated by Jews of North African origin.
MITZVAH	An action in obediance to a divine command—a good deed.

SEPHARDI	Jew of Iberian, North African or Middle Eastern origins.
SHEHITA	System of ritual slaughtering in consonance with the laws of kashrut.
SHABBAT	Jewish sabbath
SHEINE	"beautiful"
SHIKSA	non-Jewish woman
SHIVA	Judaic ritual mourning period of one week's duration.
TEFILLIN	Phylacteries; Judaic ritual objects worn by men during weekday morning prayers.
TORAH PENTATEUCH	figuratively, the Judaic legal and religious doctrine.
VAAD HA-IR	Jewish Community Council
YESHIVOT	Academies of traditional Judaic learning.
YIDDISHKAYT	Jewishness, Yiddish culture
ZAIDE	grandfather

Biographical Notes

MICHAEL BENAZON teaches literature at Champlain College, Lennoxville, Quebec.

RACHEL FELDHAY BRENNER is a professor of Hebrew at the University of Wisconsin, Madison.

MERVIN BUTOVSKY is a professor in the Department of English at Concordia University.

YOLANDE COHEN is a professor in the Département d'histoire at l'Université du Québec à Montréal.

SIMCHA FISHBANE is a professor of Jewish Studies at Touro College, New York.

JACK JEDWAB is Executive Director of the Quebec Region, Canadian Jewish Congress.

JOSEPH LEVY is a professor in the Département de sexologie at l'Université du Québec à Montréal.

IRA ROBINSON is a professor of Judaic Studies and Chair of the Department of Religion at Concordia University. He is also president of the Canadian Historical Society.

WILLIAM SHAFFIR is a professor of Sociology at McMaster University.

DOSSIER QUÉBEC SERIES

Life of the Party
GÉRARD FORTIN AND BOYCE RICHARDSON

The Milton-Park Affair: Canada's Largest Citizen-Developer Confrontation
CLAIRE HELMAN

A Man of Sentiment: The Memoirs of Philippe-Joseph Aubert de Gaspé 1786-1871
TRANSLATED AND ANNOTATED BY JANE BRIERLEY

Yellow-Wolfe & Other Tales of the Saint Lawrence
Philippe-Joseph Aubert de Gaspé
TRANSLATED BY JANE BRIERLEY

Swinging in Paradise: The Story of Jazz in Montreal
JOHN GILMORE

Who's Who of Jazz in Montreal: Ragtime to 1970
JOHN GILMORE

Grassroots, Greystones & Glass Towers: Montreal Urban Issues and Architecture
BRYAN DEMCHINSKY

An Everyday Miracle: Yiddish Culture in Montreal (o/p)
EDITED BY IRA ROBINSON, PIERRE ANCTIL, MERVIN BUTOVSKY

The Passionate Debate: The Social and Political Ideas of Quebec Nationalism 1920-1945
MICHAEL OLIVER